TICKLING THE DRAGON'S TAIL

TICKLING
—THE—
DRAGON'S
TAIL

Politicians, Bureaucrats, and Scientists in
the Nuclear Age

Jeffrey L. Kaplan

Tickling the Dragon's Tail: Politicians, Bureaucrats and Scientists in the
Nuclear Age
Jeffrey L. Kaplan

Copyediting by Sarah Kolb-Williams
Book design by Stewart Williams
Produced by Spoonbridge Press

Cover image: Bettmann via Getty Images

First U.S. Edition, 2025

Hardcover ISBN: 979-8-9928109-0-5

Paperback ISBN: 979-8-9928109-1-2

Ebook ISBN: 979-8-9928109-2-9

CONTENTS

INTRODUCTION

The impetus for writing this book came from reading the papers of a former World War II officer, which my mother had acquired at an estate sale some twenty-five years ago. The officer was a member of the survey team that determined ground zero at Hiroshima after the bombing. The papers included journal entries he made while in Japan shortly after the end of the war and commentaries he wrote some forty years later.

The officer posed two basic questions:

"Why did the United States drop the bomb on Japan?" and "How can the world avoid a nuclear war?"

Henry Stimson, who had been the secretary of war throughout the Second World War, provided an answer to the first question in an article that appeared in *Harper's Magazine* in 1947. He claimed that the only alternative to Hiroshima was an invasion of Japan that would have resulted in a million dead and wounded American soldiers. His explanation has remained the best-known account of the decision to use the atomic bomb.

But Stimson's version of events is misleading. He inflated the casualty estimate while covering over other factors that influenced the United States' decision to use the atomic bomb. Stimson's motives for this are unclear. He may have been trying to provide political cover for himself and others in the government because of moral concerns over America's use of such a terrible weapon that appeared in the press shortly after the atomic bombings of Hiroshima and Nagasaki. He may have been trying to comfort a country that needed to heal after four years of war. Or perhaps his motivation included a little of both.

By describing America's use of the atomic bomb as a necessary act that saved lives, Stimson's *Harper's* article encouraged Americans to bypass any moral examination of what their country had done. Instead, they should eagerly embrace the idea that the atomic bomb was necessary for putting an end to the brutal German and Japanese regimes that had threatened the world. The United States was the "good guy" of this story. Its people had fought the "good war," and in the decades that followed, the Americans of that time became known as the "greatest generation."

Stimson's justification for the use of the atomic bomb went virtually unchallenged for almost two decades. However, starting in the mid-1960s, a number of historians have questioned his account. One of the first was Gar Alperovitz, whose book *Atomic Diplomacy: Hiroshima and Potsdam* was published in 1965. Based on his examination of government documents and personal memoirs from key decision-makers that had only recently been made public, Alperovitz suggested that geopolitical concerns about postwar relationships with the Soviet Union played a major role in the decision.

The absence of any moral questioning during the postwar period concerning the use of the bomb made it easy to cast the Soviet Union into the role, once held by Germany and Japan, of evil empire. The Soviets were to be fought with the same resolve the greatest generation had drawn on to fight the enemies of its time, even though the advent of the hydrogen bomb in the early 1950s meant that war would now result in the death of hundreds of millions, possibly even all of humankind, not the tens of thousands it had in 1945. But America still considered itself the "good guy" who only turned to violence when it was necessary. Alperovitz's book set off a hotly contested debate among historians that continues to this day.

In 1975 Martin J. Sherwin raised similar issues in *A World Destroyed: Hiroshima and Its Legacies*. In 1995 Alperovitz used material that had become available since his first book was published to produce a much-expanded update, *The Decision to Use the Atomic Bomb*.

One of the best books of the period to defend Stimson's older narrative is Richard Frank's *Downfall: The End of the Imperial Japanese Empire*, published in 2001.

Other illuminating perspectives are provided in *The End of the Pacific War: Reappraisals* (2007), edited by Tsuyoshi Hasegawa. This book is a collection of essays by Japanese and American historians, each with a different point of view, examining the reaction of Japanese leaders to the dropping of the atomic bombs over Hiroshima and Nagasaki.

This debate among historians is important. More often than not, it is historians rather than government officials who "make" history. The historians write the books that capture the attention of the reading public and the writers of school textbooks. Yet even the most fastidious historians have to rely on conflicting evidence. First and foremost, historians typically use "primary sources," material that was created at the time of the events being described. Such sources can be official reports, diaries, letters, or recordings. Official documents often reflect internal struggles over policies and budgets. Diaries and letters from different individuals may contradict each other. Of course, historians also view the source material through the lens of their own assumptions and moral beliefs.

For these reasons, this book not only describes the actions and words of historical figures but also allows the voices of the historians themselves to be heard. Questions about the decision to use the atomic bomb are at the heart of the conflict between the traditionalists, who adhere to Stimson's account, and the revisionist historians, who claim that the reason American leaders dropped the atomic bomb on Hiroshima and Nagasaki had more to do with establishing the United States as the dominant world power after the war than it did with preventing the loss of Americans lives in an invasion of Japan. This work examines some of those conflicting accounts, especially in the chapters dealing with the decision to drop the bomb—perhaps the most fateful single decision in human history.

The "revisionist" history of the atomic bombing of Japan makes one thing clear: possessing the most powerful weapon ever developed was an irresistible attraction for America's national politicians and bureaucrats. The extent to which that attraction influenced the decision to use the atomic bomb against Japan is a major focus of this book. What is undeniable is that almost immediately after the war the United States began using the bomb to threaten other countries and has continued to do so. It is also undeniable that America's leaders looked forward to wielding its power well before the bomb was ready for use. In fact, there is considerable evidence that Hiroshima was meant to serve, at least in part, as an implicit warning to one of the United States' own wartime allies, the Soviet Union.

Later chapters examine the Cold War era and its beginnings, the Cuban Missile Crisis, and Ronald Reagan's Strategic Defense Initiative. The book then moves on to the post–Cold War era with chapters on how America's attempts to maintain its claim to being the world's sole superpower has affected its foreign policy, its domestic affairs, and the current state of the nuclear threat.

The big question that looms over all of us is the second one the officer from the Hiroshima survey team asked: How can the world avoid a nuclear war? That question is more urgent than ever. The famous Doomsday Clock maintained by the *Bulletin of the Atomic Scientists* offers a useful perspective on our current situation. The *Bulletin* was established in 1945 by scientists who helped to develop the atomic bomb. These scientists saw a vital need to help the public confront the implications of the atomic bombings of Hiroshima and Nagasaki and understand what the threat of atomic war meant for humanity. The *Bulletin*'s founders also realized that modern science would soon produce many other dangerous technologies.

In response, they created the symbolic Doomsday Clock to

illustrate how close humanity is to extinction. In the early 1990s, the *Bulletin* set the Doomsday Clock to seventeen minutes before midnight, the farthest it has ever been from the moment of catastrophe. In 2022, it was set to 90 seconds before midnight, the closest it has ever been, and it has remained at the same setting in 2024. One of the reasons is that the nuclear arms race between Russia and the United States has resumed with both sides developing weapons that pose a greater threat than ever before. Another factor is that democracy and decision-making are being undermined by the corrupting influence of disinformation campaigns on the internet. And finally, climate change looms before us, threatening to rip apart the fabric of every society on the planet. As a result, humanity is more likely than ever before to stumble into a nuclear war.

We must find a way to pull the hands of the Doomsday Clock back from midnight. But for us to have a chance of doing so, the people of the United States need to take a hard, unblinking look at their country's role in bringing the world so close to the possibility of nuclear conflagration. Perhaps this book can, in some small way, help us do just that.

CHAPTER 1

The Beginnings of Atomic Diplomacy

Truman and the Potsdam Conference, 1945—American and Soviet Discord

The rapidly changing situation during the closing months of World War II makes matters particularly challenging for a historian wishing to understand the dynamics between the major powers at the time.

The Japanese, the Americans, and the Soviets were all trying to adjust as events unfolded because those adjustments would have consequences for both the conduct of the war's final days and the geopolitical situation after the war. What one can say with certainty is that all of those dynamics changed when Harry S. Truman became president of the United States. Franklin D. Roosevelt died suddenly on April 12, 1945; a few hours later Vice President Harry S. Truman was sworn in as president. He was ill-prepared for the task, and he knew it. When Truman assumed the presidency, he had been vice president for less than three months. Party leaders had persuaded Roosevelt to drop his previous vice president, Henry Wallace, for the 1944 elections because they considered him too supportive of labor. They chose Truman, who had been a senator from Missouri for the past eleven years, in what some members of

Congress jokingly called the "Missouri Compromise," referring to a pre–Civil War agreement regarding slavery.[1]

By his own estimate, Truman met with President Roosevelt only twice during his time as vice president and perhaps half a dozen times during the previous nine months. Roosevelt told him almost nothing about the progress of the war or the agreements the United States had made with its allies. Nor did Truman know anything about the atomic bomb.[2] Moreover, Truman was emotionally unprepared to become president, despite the well-known fact that Roosevelt's health was fragile. Truman wrote in his memoirs, "I had been afraid for many weeks that something might happen to this great leader, but . . . I did not allow myself to think about it after I became Vice-President." His image as a tough, confident leader was one Truman had carefully cultivated.[3]

On May 8, less than a month after Truman assumed the presidency, the Allies declared victory in Europe. At that point, the major tasks for the new president were to defeat Japan and set the stage for postwar relations with the Soviet Union. The context for both of these issues had been reached the previous February when Roosevelt, Churchill, and Stalin met at Yalta in Crimea. By the time of the Yalta Conference, it was clear Germany would soon surrender, but victory over Japan did not appear imminent.

A major goal of Roosevelt and Churchill at Yalta was to get Stalin to end Russian neutrality regarding Japan and enter the war in the Far East. Stalin agreed to do so within three months of Germany's surrender. In return, the Soviet Union would reclaim territory near Japan that it had once held, two seaports along the China coast, and partial control of the railroads in Manchuria. Those agreements also involved a set of concessions for Soviet spheres of influence in Eastern Europe in exchange for similar areas of U.S. and British control in other areas such as Italy and Greece.[4]

The agreements reached at Yalta regarding Eastern Europe were ambiguous. At the time of the conference, Stalin's forces controlled much of Eastern Europe. As Truman's closest advisor, James F. Byrnes, put it: "It was not a question of what we would *let* the Russians do, but what we could *get* [italics in the original] the Russians to do."[5] The Soviets agreed to a vague public statement that they would guarantee "interim governmental authorities [who were] broadly representative of all democratic elements in the population and . . . the earliest possible establishment [of] free elections of governments [that were] responsive to the will of the people." The declaration specifically mentioned that "the provisional government which is now functioning in Poland should therefore be reorganized on a broader democratic basis with the inclusion of democratic leaders from Poland itself and from Poles abroad."[6] Roosevelt had built a strong personal relationship with Stalin, and this may have led him to believe it would be possible to work things through with Stalin in the future.

The vagueness of the Russian claim left a lot of room for subsequent disagreements and mistrust between the Soviets, the United States, and Britain.[7] Shortly before Truman became president, tensions developed between the United States and the Soviet Union over which groups of Polish politicians would be responsive to "the will of the people." The Russians were intent on establishing a permanent government that would be largely under their control, while the United States wanted one that would be more aligned with Western Europe. At Yalta, Roosevelt and Churchill had given extra assurances to the Soviets regarding Poland, stating that Poland's government would be "friendly" to the Soviet Union. Roosevelt understood Poland was, as Stalin later declared, the country the Soviet Union was "interested in first of all and most of all" because the main thrust of Hitler's invasion of the Soviet Union had come through Poland.[8]

In fact, shortly before he died, Roosevelt responded to Churchill's attempts to press Stalin on the Polish issue by reminding Churchill that "we placed, as clearly shown in the agreement, somewhat more emphasis . . . on [Soviet-oriented Polish politicians in the government]."[9] Roosevelt's personal diplomacy died with him. Now Truman found himself faced with a group of hard-line advisors who were suspicious of the Soviets, the American ambassador to the Soviet Union Averell Harriman, Secretary of State Edward Stettinius, and Admiral James Forrestal among them. These hard-liners who had Truman's ear were convinced Stalin wanted to expand Russian control to as much of Eastern Europe as he could get his hands on.[10] As Harriman put it, "The Soviet program is the establishment of totalitarianism, ending personal liberty and democracy as we know and respect it."[11]

Truman had no experience with diplomacy, personal or otherwise. As Martin J. Sherwin writes in *A World Destroyed: Hiroshima and Its Legacies* (2003):

> The suddenness of Roosevelt's passing thus effectively left policymaking in the hands of his inherited advisers, who, for the most part, viewed Soviet intentions in a more sinister light than Roosevelt had. . . . They easily persuaded Truman to adopt a harsher, less conciliatory stance toward the Russians than his predecessor had pursued.[12]

Others took a more conciliatory position. Secretary of War Henry Stimson pointed out that Stalin had always kept his word on military matters and often exceeded his commitments. Admiral William Leahy, who was the highest-ranking military officer and had been Roosevelt's personal chief of staff, pointed to the ambiguity of the Yalta Agreements and believed there was room for negotiation.

Of course, there were plenty of reasons to suspect Stalin's motives. He was a brutal, paranoid authoritarian who had killed millions of ordinary Soviet citizens, as well as many government officials who fell into his disfavor. But Roosevelt and Churchill understood that Stalin had legitimate concerns about the Soviet Union's borders with Europe. The roots of Stalin's concerns extended back to the nineteenth century; 125 years earlier, Napoleon invaded Russia through Poland, the shortest route from Western Europe to Saint Petersburg (later Leningrad) and Moscow.

Stalin also had ample reason to mistrust Truman personally. As a senator, Truman had responded to the news of Germany's 1941 invasion of the Soviet Union by declaring, "If we see that Germany is winning the war we ought to help Russia and if Russia is winning we ought to help Germany and that way let them kill as many as possible."[13] To Stalin, Truman's hostility likely appeared in keeping with America's military intervention in 1918 when the U.S. sent 13,000 American troops to fight against the Bolshevists during the Russian Civil War.[14]

At the urging of Soviet Ambassador Harriman, Admiral Leahy, and others who believed blunt language "would have a beneficial effect on the Soviet outlook," Truman pursued a "showdown" over Poland with the Soviet Ambassador Vyacheslav Molotov.[15]

The meeting with Molotov took place on April 23, 1945. In an atmosphere of mutual suspicion, the two allies berated each other. Molotov insisted the Soviets were following the Yalta Agreements, while Truman claimed they were proceeding on the basis of "a one-way street." Molotov responded, "I have never been talked to like that in my life." Truman replied, "Carry out your agreements and you won't get talked to like that."[16]

The results of this meeting were not what Truman expected. The Soviets proved to be unmovable on the issue of Poland, even after the U.S. tried to pressure them regarding American economic aid for the Soviet war effort. Stalin remained firm on his insistence that Poland's government be controlled by Russia. Truman backed down on his Polish demands.

In the days that followed, Truman agreed with Harriman that another three-way meeting between Truman, Churchill, and Stalin was needed to establish "a basis for future relations with Russia" and "the longer the meeting was delayed the worse the situation would get," and "if the meeting could take place before we were in a large measure out of Europe . . . the atmosphere of the meeting would be more favorable [to the U.S. and the West] and the chances of success increased."[17]

The scheduled meeting became known as the Potsdam Conference, named after the German city adjacent to Berlin where it was held. Truman chose to delay the meeting to mid-July. That decision became a critical inflection point for understanding both the decision to use the atomic bomb and future relations with the Soviet Union.

It is not surprising that Truman, suddenly thrust into enormous responsibility over complex issues of which he had little knowledge, sought a trusted advisor he had known before he became president. That advisor was James F. Byrnes.

Byrnes had been an influential senator from South Carolina (elected in 1932) and a prominent supporter of the New Deal. In 1941, Roosevelt appointed him to the U.S. Supreme Court, where he served for fifteen months before resigning to join the Roosevelt administration. He soon became head of the Office of War Mobilization that oversaw the wartime economy. Byrnes had also served as Truman's mentor when the future president was first elected to the Senate. As one historian commented, "Truman held him in the sort of awe a younger sibling feels toward a more experienced and more talented older brother."[18]

Truman told Byrnes in mid-April of 1945 that he wanted him to become his secretary of state, and he appointed Byrnes to the position in July. Since there was no vice president, the law governing succession at the time made Byrnes the next in line to become president. In early May, Truman made Byrnes his personal representative on the Interim Committee, the obscurely named high-level group in charge of oversight for the program to develop the atomic bomb. The bomb development program was referred to by government officials who knew of its existence as the Manhattan Project. Byrnes became the only advisor to the president who was closely involved with both foreign policy and oversight of the development of the atomic bomb.

Another important consideration for Truman was that Byrnes had accompanied Roosevelt to the Yalta Conference. Byrnes had attended many of the discussions between the leaders and had taken notes. Since there was no official transcript or other account of the discussions that had led to the formal agreements, Byrne's perspective on what had happened at Yalta would likely have carried a great deal of weight with Truman.[19] He knew such knowledge would be extremely useful at Potsdam, which, after all, was intended to be a follow-up to Yalta.

Given their long-standing personal relationship and Byrne's experience in domestic and foreign politics, "immediately upon becoming President, I sent for him because I wanted his assistance."[20] He met with Byrnes starting the day after Roosevelt's death, and Byrnes appears to have been deeply involved in policy consultations with Truman from that point on. Byrnes had a central role in guiding Truman in his dealings with Stalin, and after becoming secretary of state on July 3, 1945, he helped Truman prepare for the Potsdam Conference. Byrnes played an important role in the decision to postpone the Potsdam Conference in the hope that the United States could enter the negotiations knowing the atomic bomb had been successfully tested.[21]

Secretary of War Stimson also advocated postponing the Potsdam Conference. In a meeting in mid-May of 1945. Secretary of State Stettinius (who was still secretary of state at that point), Secretary of the Navy Forrestal, Ambassador Harriman, and other advisors wanted an immediate confrontation with the Soviets regarding the future of Eastern Europe. But Stimson argued for the meeting with Churchill and Stalin to be delayed: "Over any such tangled weave of problems, [the atomic-bomb] secret would be dominant, and yet we will not know . . . whether this is a weapon in our hands or not. . . . It seems a terrible thing to gamble with such big stakes in diplomacy without having your master card in your hand."[22]

Stimson's logic in waiting for the bomb was not so that it could be used as a diplomatic cudgel to force Stalin to make broad concessions. Instead, he felt the United States needed to bring the Soviets into some sort of international system of control over nuclear technology. He believed the United States could not maintain sole control of nuclear weaponry for long; attempting to do so would lead to an arms race. Stimson noted, "The future may see a time when such a weapon may be constructed in secret and used suddenly and effectively with devastating power by a willful nation or group against an unsuspecting nation."[23] Instead, he thought the United States should offer to take the Russians into an atomic "partnership" in exchange for a diplomatic settlement of "Polish, Rumanian, [and] Yugoslavian . . . problems."[24]

Secretary of State Byrnes had a very different view of the matter. He told Truman the atomic bomb would allow the United States "to dictate our own terms at the end of the war."[25]

With the expectation that the bomb would be successfully tested in July, Truman cabled Churchill to let him know he could not meet with Stalin until that time.[26] Because the existence of the Manhattan Project was known to only a few people in the government, Truman told Ambassador Harriman and other advisors who did not know about the project that he needed to deal with the budget before meeting with Churchill and Stalin. He reassured Churchill that the U.S. would maintain its troop presence in Europe well beyond July.

Before the conference, Truman suggested to Stalin that a compromise on Poland might be possible through further negotiations.[27] This negotiation offer was in keeping with the other delaying tactics Truman used through the first several days of the

Potsdam Conference itself until he heard the news that the atomic bomb test in New Mexico had been a success.

While the primary concern over Europe was about its future, the overriding issue for the present was the war with Japan, still very much underway. But even there, the diplomatic issues were entangled with military ones. As had been the case at Yalta, the question of Russian intervention against Japan was to be a major focus of American strategy during the Potsdam Conference.

At the time of the Yalta Conference, the United States saw a Russian attack against Japan as essential for bringing about a Japanese surrender in the near term. However, in February of 1945, Stalin was still focused on what amounted to an existential struggle with the Germans. He agreed at that time, however, to disavow the neutrality agreement he had entered into with the Japanese and attack them within three months of Germany's surrender.

By May 1945, American leaders were becoming less certain they would need the Soviets' help to defeat Japan. Having broken the Japanese code early in the war, the United States knew in mid-April that Japan was looking for a way to surrender. Japan's military situation had been steadily deteriorating as American forces pressed ever closer to Japan's mainland. In June, the Japanese foreign minister Tōgō was authorized to approach the Soviet Union, hoping Stalin would act as an intermediary in surrender negotiations with the United States. The main sticking point for the Japanese was that the United States demanded "unconditional surrender," [28] which seemed to imply that the U.S. might dethrone the emperor or even hang him. Japan's leaders saw this as a threat to Japan's existence as a nation.

American leaders understood very well that the emperor was viewed as a god. Most Japanese people had never been allowed to hear his voice or gaze at his person. A 1944 study authorized by General MacArthur stated,

> To dethrone, or hang, the Emperor would cause a tremendous

and violent reaction from all Japanese. Hanging of the Emperor to them would be comparable to the crucifixion of Christ to us. All would fight to die like ants. . . . The war would be unduly prolonged; our losses heavier than otherwise would be necessary.[29]

A memorandum to the president by the War Department's Office of Operations confirmed this assessment in June 1945:

Every evidence, without exception, that we are able to obtain of the views of the Japanese with regard to the institution of the throne, indicates that the non-molestation of the person of the present emperor and the preservation of the institution of the throne comprise irreducible Japanese terms. . . . Failure on our part to clarify our intentions in this regard . . . will ensure prolongation of the war and cost a large number of human lives.[30]

The first atomic test occurred on July 16, 1945, the day before the Potsdam Conference opened. Two days later, July 18, Truman was told that the test of the atomic bomb in Alamogordo, New Mexico, had been a success. On July 16, 1945, a sequence of events began that shows how deeply concerned the military leaders of the States and Great Britain were that failure to assure the safety of the emperor would prolong the war unnecessarily. The U.S. Chiefs of Staff requested that the British military chiefs ask Churchill to bring up the issue of the surrender terms with Truman. The next day, July 17, General Sir Hastings Ismay, chief of staff to Britain's minister of defense, delivered a note directly to Churchill stating that

the Combined Chiefs of Staff . . . suggested that if and when Russia came into the war against Japan, the Japanese would probably wish to get out on almost any terms short of the dethronement of the Emperor [and that the] United States Chiefs of Staff . . . asked whether you yourself would be prepared to raise the point with the President.[31]

On July 18, Churchill did indeed raise the issue with Truman:

I dwelt upon the tremendous cost in American life and, to a smaller extent, in British life which would be involved in forcing "unconditional surrender" upon the Japanese. It was for him [Truman] to consider whether this might not be expressed in some other way, so that we got all the essentials for future peace and security.[32]

On July 21, Truman received a full report detailing just how powerful the bomb had been. At that point, he became far more assertive with Stalin at the conference in an attempt to roll back some of the concessions Roosevelt had made at Yalta regarding Eastern Europe. According to Stimson's diaries, Churchill noticed "Truman was evidently much fortified by something that had happened and that he stood up to the Russians in a most emphatic and decisive manner."[33]

Upon learning of the atomic bomb report the next day, Secretary of State Stimson quoted Churchill as saying, "Now I know what happened to Truman yesterday . . . after having read this report he was a changed man. He told the Russians just where they got on and off and generally bossed the whole meeting." Stimson also noted that Churchill said he felt the same way after learning the news.[34]

Truman did make one conciliatory gesture toward Stalin. In mid-June, the Interim Committee decided that if the Russians were not informed about the bomb, and if the U.S. were to use it a few weeks later, distrust might make it difficult to gain their cooperation in future nuclear arms agreements.[35] Truman followed this advice in a purposely vague manner:

I casually mentioned to Stalin that we had a new weapon of unusual destructive force. The Russian Premier showed no special interest. All he said was that he was glad to hear it and hoped we would make "good use of it" against the Japanese.[36]

As it was, Stalin knew a good deal more about the Manhattan Project than Truman realized. Soviet spies had been updating the Soviets on a regular basis, although it is not clear how much importance Stalin attached to Truman's statement at the time.[37]

Secretary of State Byrnes was surprised by Stalin's seeming indifference to Truman's message concerning a new weapon. Messer suggests that Byrnes must have concluded,

The overriding significance of the atomic bomb would only sink into the remarkably obtuse Soviet consciousness after its power had been demonstrated in combat against Japan. Then surely the Russians would acknowledge the primacy of the bomb as the controlling force in postwar international relations.[38]

Since Stalin had firmly resisted all of Truman's demands concerning Eastern Europe and the world had not yet seen the bomb in action, Truman simply left those issues for later. However, he and Churchill took one more step that further undermined their relationship with Stalin and may have helped prolong the war with Japan.

Negotiations: The Russian Invasion and the Surrender of Japan

In the weeks leading up to Potsdam, American officials had concluded that the three participants at Potsdam should deliver a joint surrender ultimatum to the Japanese. The Americans also considered including the "ominous threat of Russia" in the declaration. But after learning of the full power of the atomic bomb, Truman decided to eliminate the Soviets from the proclamation.[39]

On July 26, 1945, the United States and Britain, in conjunction with China (which had no representatives at Potsdam), issued their surrender ultimatum to Japan without any assurances about the emperor's safety. They did not inform Stalin beforehand. This ultimatum became known as the Potsdam Declaration, also known as the Potsdam Proclamation. (The Potsdam Declaration was an entirely different document than the official Potsdam Agreement, which was issued on August 2, 1945, and signed by Stalin, Churchill, and Truman and dealt with the issues for which the conference was convened: the postwar future of Europe.)

On July 28, 1945, two days after the Potsdam Declaration, Soviet Ambassador Molotov suggested the United States, England, and "other allies in the Far Eastern War" send a "formal request to the Soviet government for its entry into the war" based on Japan's refusal to accept the surrender ultimatum.[40] The American response to Molotov's suggestion was to send a confusing, legalistic letter to Stalin that neither accepted Molotov's proposal nor explicitly rejected it. Byrnes was quite clear on why the Soviets had been eliminated from the Potsdam Declaration: "We did not want to urge the Russians to enter the war."[41]

Yet two weeks earlier, after a preconference meeting with Stalin at Potsdam on July 17, Truman wrote in his journal that Stalin would enter the war against Japan by August 15, and that the Japanese would be finished. The day after the Potsdam Declaration, Truman wrote to his wife,

I've gotten what I came for—Stalin goes to war on August 15 with no strings on it. . . . I'll say that we'll end the war a year sooner now, and think of the kids who won't be killed! That is the important thing.[42]

By the time of the conference, Truman also knew that the Japanese had intensified their efforts to work through Stalin as an intermediary to end the war with the United States. Emperor Hirohito had informed the Soviets that for the first time he was sending them an envoy "at the particular desire of his Majesty."[43] Clearly, Truman must have understood that had the Soviets declared their intention to enter the war in the Far East, the Japanese would have realized their situation was more dire than they thought. He must have also realized that if the threat from the Soviet Union was combined with surrender terms that included allowing the Japanese throne to survive in some form, an early surrender might well have been more likely. But Truman and many of his advisors were anxious to reverse the secret agreements Roosevelt had made with Stalin at Yalta. These agreements would have created a Soviet sphere of influence in the Far East in exchange for Soviet help in defeating Japan. The Soviets were to take over the Kuril Islands north of Japan, then gain control of Outer Mongolia and partial control of railroads in Manchuria. They would also regain control of two ports on the China coast that they had lost forty years earlier in the Russo–Japanese War.

Upon learning of the successful atomic bomb test, Truman and Byrnes orchestrated a delaying tactic involving China and its leader, Chiang Kai-shek. The Chinese were engaged in negotiations with the Soviets over the conduct of the Soviet invasion of Japanese-held territory in China and the Soviet advance through China toward Japan itself. The Americans urged the Chinese to draw out these negotiations as best they could until they heard from Washington. Truman and Byrnes were playing a cat-and-mouse game with Stalin. Truman wasn't absolutely sure an atomic bomb attack would succeed, but he was confident that a Soviet invasion would end the war quickly.[44] Byrnes was "still hoping for time, believing that after [the] atomic bomb Japan will surrender and Russia will not get in so much on the kill, [nor would they be in] a position to press for claims against China."[45]

The dual objectives of assuring Soviet entry while containing Soviet expansion were clearly not contradictory to Truman. As Truman put it a decade later, "One of the main objectives of the Potsdam Conference [was] to get Russia in as quickly as we could and then to keep Russia out of Japan—and I did it." Although he saw the bomb as useful for ending the war before the Soviets could claim credit for the victory, Truman apparently wasn't ready to rely totally on the bomb until it was proven in combat.[46] Truman's diary entry from Potsdam records a comment he made to Churchill: "[The Japanese] will fold up before Russia comes in. I am sure they will when Manhattan appears over their homeland."[47]

Historian Robert Messer notes that

> The implications of these passages from Truman's diary and letters for the orthodox defense of the bomb's use are devastating. If Soviet entry alone would end the war before an invasion of Japan, the use of atomic bombs cannot be justified as the only alternative to that invasion.[48]

A Russian invasion would have meant the war would be over in a matter of days. The decision to use the bomb was driven not by military necessity alone, but also by concerns about how the bomb might be used to affect the balance of power after the war. In essence, America's leaders were fighting a future cold war against a country that was its ally in a still-ongoing hot war.

Of course, Truman and his advisors could not have known for certain how the Japanese would react to any course of action they chose. Earlier warnings by General MacArthur in 1944 concerning the harming or deposing the emperor appear to have been cast aside in favor of postwar global political strategy. In 1965, the important question regarding Truman's decision to use the atomic bomb is not whether a modification of the surrender terms would have been sufficient to elicit a Japanese surrender without a Russian invasion. Rather, as Alperovitz suggested in his 1965 book *Atomic Diplomacy*, "It is not my purpose to argue whether either or both of these measures would, in fact, have ended the war. What I wished to show is that American leaders *believed* [italics in the original] such a result was likely" and that as early as April 18, intelligence and military advisors reported that "either a Russian declaration of war or a change in the surrender terms was likely to bring capitulation."[49]

Counterfactual speculations, the what-ifs of history, can lead to endless debate. That has certainly been the case regarding the Japanese surrender at the end of World War II. The problem is that Japan's leaders did not agree on what "the preservation of the emperor system" actually entailed.

JAPANESE DEMANDS IN THE SURRENDER TERMS

The traditionalist account of how the decision to use the atomic bomb was made leans heavily on the notion that after Hiroshima and Nagasaki, the Japanese realized they had no alternative other than to surrender. But even the traditionalists have had to admit that the atomic bomb was not the only event that pushed Japan's leaders toward surrender. On August 9, three days after the bombing of Hiroshima, Japan's leaders learned that the Soviet Union had declared war against their country and the Soviet army would be at Japan's northern border in a matter of days.

The close juxtaposition of these events sparked the debate over which one was decisive in Japan's decision to surrender. If the traditionalists can show that the atomic bomb was the most important consideration, it would help justify its use. On the other hand, if the Soviet invasion was the most important factor, it would tend to support the revisionist view that dropping the bomb was unnecessary.

It would also support the revisionist argument that excluding the Soviet Union from the Potsdam Declaration prolonged the war by leading the Japanese to believe it was worth their while to continue appealing to Stalin to intercede with the United States for more favorable surrender terms than those demanded by the Declaration.

The debate between the traditionalists and the revisionists centers on the complex dynamics between Emperor Hirohito, the Japanese cabinet, and the six military officers who comprised Japan's Supreme Council for the Direction of the War, which was to have the final authority to decide whether to surrender or continue the war. The six members of the Supreme Council, often called the Big Six in historical accounts, were Prime Minister Suzuki Kantarō, Foreign Minister Tōgō Shigenori, Army Minister Anami Korechika, Navy Minister Yonai Misumasa, Army Chief of Staff Umezu Yoshijiro, and Navy Chief of Staff Toyoda Soemu. Other significant figures included Prince Fumimaro Konoe, a member of the royal family, as well as the Lord Keeper of the Privy Seal Kōichi Kido, who also served as the principal advisor to the emperor.

The Supreme Council's decisions had to be unanimous and approved by the government's cabinet. However, any of the four military members of the Big Six could force the dissolution of the cabinet. This necessity for unanimity among the Big Six led to a stalemate in the closing days of the war because they could not agree on the surrender terms among themselves. In the end, it was the emperor who broke with tradition and made the final decision to end the war.

In one of the essays in Tsuyoshi Hasegawa's *The End of the Pacific War: Reappraisals* (2007), the historian Sumio Hatano lays out a useful chronology of events among the Japanese officials involved, while Hasegawa provides an insightful analysis of those events.

Around noon on August 7, 1945, the day after the atomic bomb was detonated over Japan, Lord Keeper of the Privy Seal Kido received a report that the United States had used an atomic bomb against the city of Hiroshima, inflicting enormous casualties of about 130,000 people. At a cabinet meeting that day, Foreign Minister Tōgō suggested that "atomic bombs may trigger revolutionary changes in the war."[50] The next morning, Tōgō urged the emperor to end the war.

The emperor concluded that the "arrival of that sort of new weapon now makes it impossible to continue the war," and he directed Foreign Minister Tōgō to "exert every effort to terminate the war without delay" and to inform Prime Minister Suzuki of his decision.[51]

For his part, Prime Minister Suzuki believed the bomb was a "very suitable excuse" for beginning "peace parleys"[52] and attempted to set up a meeting of the Big Six for August 8. However, he was unable to do so because the military leaders claimed they had "prior commitments." Hasegawa suggests that "this laxity is indicative of the way the ruling elite felt regarding the 'shock' of the Hiroshima bomb."[53]

But the military leaders displayed a newfound sense of urgency with the Soviets' entry into the war the next day. At around 4:00 a.m. on August 9, the Japanese learned that the Soviet Union had declared war against Japan and its troops were advancing through Manchuria toward Japan. At that point, Foreign Minister Tōgō urged the Big Six to agree to the surrender terms of the Potsdam Declaration with the added condition that the emperor's position would be preserved.

Prime Minister Suzuki reached a similar conclusion: "The Soviet entry into the war meant the collapse of peace negotiations through Soviet mediation, the most important policy of the cabinet." Having decided to surrender under the terms of the Potsdam Declaration, Suzuki went to the Imperial Palace, where Lord Keeper of the Privy Seal Kido relayed his decision to the emperor. Kido reported back that the emperor agreed with Suzuki's surrender plan. Suzuki then set up the meeting of the Big Six, which began on August 9 at 10:30 a.m.[54]

When the Big Six met to decide on terms for the surrender, Prime Minister Suzuki stated, "We have been hit hard by the atomic bombing of Hiroshima. Now we have the Soviet entry into the war. It has become almost impossible to continue the war [and] we seem to have no other choice but to accept the Potsdam Proclamation."[55] Before Japan's complete surrender, Suzuki proposed four points for discussion: (1) the preservation of the emperor system, (2) the disarmament of the Japanese Armed Forces, (3) the issue of war criminals, and (4) the details of postwar military occupation.

The Council was divided. Anami, Umezu, and Toyoda insisted the Japanese military must be allowed to disarm themselves. They argued that Japan would punish any war criminals on its own, and that there should be no military occupation of the homeland.

When Foreign Minister Tōgō pointed out that the Americans were unlikely to accept these terms, Anami and Umezu declared that if they didn't, they would attempt a "single and decisive blow" against an American invasion of Japan: "Though the odds of ultimately winning are against us, we can still put up a last-ditch fight."[56] The name for this plan was "Ketsu Gō."[57]

Even though the news of the atomic bombing at Nagasaki on August 9 arrived during the meeting, Hatano notes that "it did not significantly alter the course of discussion" of the surrender terms. Only Navy Minister Yonai, who saw the atomic bombs and the Soviet attack as a "gift from Heaven" and a way to end the war, agreed with Tōgō's position that the sole condition should be preserving "the safety of the imperial family."[58]

The Big Six then met with the full cabinet at 2:30 in the afternoon of August 9. Discussion topics included concerns that the public was losing trust in the military and even the emperor system itself.[59] The stalemate on surrender terms continued until the meeting was suspended shortly after 10:00 p.m. without any resolution.[60]

Earlier that afternoon, Kido had a meeting with Emperor

Hirohito at which the emperor made a "sacred decision" that Japan must surrender. On learning of the emperor's decision, Suzuki arranged for the emperor to be present when the Big Six meeting resumed shortly before midnight on August 9.[61]

At that meeting, Foreign Minister Tōgō insisted that they should make the "preservation and safety of the emperor's family the only condition." Again, Anami and Umezu insisted that all four conditions were "absolutely essential" for the continuance of the imperial system. Only when the emperor endorsed the decision to surrender with the single provision did Japan cable its message of surrender to the United States via the Swiss and Swedish governments in the early morning of August 10.[62]

Although there is little dispute about the basic chronology laid out by Hatano's essay, many of the participants in the surrender negotiations wrote their own diaries and memoirs and recounted their recollection of events to American interviewers after the war. As a result, other historians have drawn very different conclusions about what was really going on behind the scenes during the meetings with the Big Six, the cabinet, and the emperor. Personal diaries and memoirs can be misleading, especially when historians use those diaries and memoirs to reinforce a particular point of view in a way that ignores the broader context of events.

For example, Richard Frank, in his essay in *The End of the Pacific War* (2007), cites Suzuki's December 1945 elaboration of comments he'd made a few days after the Japanese surrender. The former Japanese prime minister said that the Japanese military dropped their plans for "fighting a decisive battle" against an American invasion once the atomic bomb had been used. The military leaders "believed the United States would no longer attempt to land when it had such a superior weapon . . . so at that point they decided that it would be best to sue for peace."[63]

This passage, Frank claims, shows that "by any reasonable standard, the atomic bombs were essential to obtain the emperor's intervention as the essential first step to ending the war." He also claims that "in the eyes of the Big Six, the bombs also negated a plan by Japan's military resistance to an American land invasion of Japan (known as the "Ketsu Gō" strategy)"[64]

However, Frank ignores the fact that the military leaders did not see fit to cancel whatever "prior commitments" they may have had when they first heard that the United States had used its "superior weapon" against Hiroshima. They also seem to have been unmoved when they received word of the atomic bombing of Nagasaki during the Big Six meeting on August 9. The military insisted upon continuing the Ketsu Gō strategy despite the fact that Anami is known to have "made startling assertions that the United States might possess more than 100 atomic bombs, and that the next target might be Tokyo."[65]

The sequence of events immediately after the cabinet meeting on the morning of August 7 also undermines Frank's argument. Foreign Minister Tōgō sent an urgent telegram to the Japanese ambassador in Moscow after the bomb was used against Hiroshima, hoping that Stalin would finally intercede with the Americans to obtain better surrender terms for Japan than those demanded in the Potsdam Declaration. It said, "The situation is becoming more and more pressing. We must know the Soviets' attitude immediately. Therefore, do your best once more to obtain their reply immediately." Of course, two days later, the Japanese received a reply in the form of a Soviet declaration of war and a Soviet army that was rapidly advancing across northern China toward the Japanese homeland. Only after hearing of the Soviet invasion did both Tōgō and Suzuki decide it was necessary to accept the terms of the Potsdam Declaration.[66]

Hasegawa offers his own conclusions about the reasons for the Japanese surrender. Referring to the factions of the Japanese leaders that favored surrendering to the United States versus continuing the war, "Kido stated that while the peace party and the war party had previously been equally balanced on the scale, the atomic bomb helped to tip the balance in favor of the peace party." But, Hasegawa adds, "It would be more accurate to say that the Soviet entry into the war [added] to that tipped scale, then completely toppled the scale itself."[67]

Although Hatano believes the atomic bombs and the Soviet entry into the war were of equal importance, he makes several points that help bolster Hasegawa's conclusions that the Soviet invasion was the decisive factor in Japan's decision to surrender. Senior officials were also becoming increasingly alarmed over deteriorating support for the war and potentially the emperor system itself. He quotes Navy Minister Yonai:

> I have been insisting on the early settlement of the situation for a long time, but not because of my fear of the enemy's attack, the atomic bombs, or the Soviet entry into the war. It is first and foremost because of my great anxiety about the domestic situation. Therefore, it is now rather fortuitous for us to settle the situation without that matter coming to surface.[68]

But other members of the Japanese leadership worried how the military would react to any early termination of the war. When told of the Soviet entry into the war, Prince Konoe said, "It may be [a] gift from heaven for containing the army."[69] Hatano summarized the situation confronting the Japanese peace faction:

> In short, the leadership had been facing the dilemma that a hasty termination of the war might invite an army rebellion, while the protracted continuation of the war would provoke public hostility to the emperor system. The double-shocks of . . . the atomic bombs and the Soviet entry presented themselves as nothing less than a "gift from heaven" to the leadership in escaping from this dilemma. The problem, however,

lay in the fact that the Potsdam Proclamation included no reassurance from the Allied Powers on the preservation of the emperor system.[70]

Hasegawa also gives a nuanced evaluation of how the surrender terms and Truman's diplomatic moves at Potsdam affected Japan's behavior toward the end of the war. Although he remains leery of any historical counterfactual speculations, the what-ifs, he does suggest that Japan might have surrendered earlier if "Truman had asked Stalin to join the Potsdam Proclamation *and* [italics in the original] retained the promise . . . to allow the preservation of a constitutional monarchy." Doing so might "have strengthened the resolve of the peace party to seek the termination of the war, and would have made it easier for it to accept the terms, knowing that a monarchical system would be preserved and that Moscow might be harsher and demand the elimination of the emperor system. . . . In this sense, the revisionist historians' claims that the atomic bomb delayed rather than hastened Japan's surrender merits serious consideration."[71]

Hasegawa's and Hatano's assessments are consistent with comments the acting Secretary of State Joseph Grew made to Truman in mid-June of 1945 suggesting that the surrender demands should include a clarification concerning the emperor's continued status, and that this should be done before the meeting at Potsdam because "the sooner we can get the Japanese thinking about surrender" and allow time "for a peace movement to get started the better it will be and the more lives of Americans may ultimately be saved."[72] Grew had been the ambassador to Japan from 1933 until the day of Japan's attack against Pearl Harbor on December 7, 1941.

Alperovitz, on the other hand, appears to have changed his original interpretation. As previously noted, Alperovitz stated in 1965 that the important issue he was addressing was not whether the Japanese would have, in fact, surrendered without the use of the bomb if the United States had softened the surrender terms to include keeping the emperor. Rather, it was that most American officials *believed* they would have surrendered. Thirty years later in *The Decision to Use the Bomb*, Alperovitz tries to show that the Japanese would indeed have surrendered before the Hiroshima bombing had the surrender terms included keeping the emperor in place. He asserts, "He compares the disagreement among the Japanese leaders to a mundane American reference point: "hard-fought labor negotiation" where a "comparison of the proposals [is] stated by the contending parties before the beginning of bargaining."[73] Yet, in the end, the Japanese leadership could not agree among themselves about the surrender terms without the unprecedented intercession of the emperor.

In its acceptance of Japan's surrender offer, the United States included a carefully couched provision indicating that the person of the emperor would not be harmed: "From the moment of surrender the authority of the Emperor and the Japanese Government to rule the state shall be subject to the Supreme Commander of the Allied powers who will take such steps as he deems proper to effectuate the surrender terms."[74] To the war faction such reassurances were entirely insufficient.

On August 14 there was still another crisis with the cabinet and the Big Six. Once more, the emperor intervened to insist they accept the American surrender terms. At this point, General Umezu and Army Minister Anami, having acceded to the emperor's wishes, acted to thwart a coup by high-ranking military officers still hostile to the idea of surrender.

The next day, dissident army officers burned Prime Minister Suzuki's house, and General Anami committed suicide.[75] Anami's suicide was bound with his sense of honor and loyalty to Emperor Hirohito, the embodiment of the Japanese people. Overriding the emperor's decision would have been tantamount to Anami himself doing what he feared the Americans were going to do—destroy the imperial system. Caught between surrendering on what he considered unfavorable terms and the wishes of the emperor, Anami believed that the only honorable course was traditional suicide.

Frank and Alperovitz both attempted to impose their own logic on Japan's military leaders. But those leaders weren't using Frank's "reasonable standard," nor were they engaged in Alperovitz's "labor negotiation." They were willing to continue a war against a country armed with atomic weapons, even though it would result in the deaths of tens of thousands of Japanese soldiers and civilians. Anami and his colleagues were not concerned with such calculations. These military leaders were using a logic of their own. They were fighting to the death for a Japan that was the worldly manifestation of their highest principles and beliefs.

THE MORAL QUESTION OF THE BOMB

Both the traditionalists and the revisionists sometimes appear driven to create seamless opposing narratives that show no disjunction between the decision to use the atomic bomb against Japan and the question of whether or not the bomb was decisive in bringing about Japan's surrender. Yet there is no intrinsic link between those two issues. Truman's motives for dropping the atomic bomb do not bear directly on whether or not the bomb was actually the deciding factor that led to the Japanese surrender. The need for such a seamless narrative seems to be a product of moral concerns.

Carl Spaatz, the commanding general of the U.S. Army Strategic Air Force and the person who received the direct order to drop the bombs on Hiroshima and Nagasaki, recalled that at the time he "didn't think the atomic bomb was necessary" and thought "this was going to be a terrific black mark on our character." Spaatz had received verbal orders to drop the bomb but demanded they be in writing.[76] Spaatz's view that the use of the atomic bomb was not a military necessity was widely shared by other military leaders. Perhaps the most famous response was that of Dwight Eisenhower. Eisenhower, who, like many other senior military officers, believed "Japan was already defeated," recalled his thoughts upon hearing Secretary of War Stimson tell him about the plan to use the atomic bomb: "It wasn't necessary to hit them with that awful thing."[77] In his 1948 book *Crusade in Europe*, Eisenhower writes:

> I expressed the hope that we would never have to use such a thing [the atomic bomb] against any enemy because I disliked seeing the United States take the lead in introducing into war something as horrible and destructive as this new weapon was described to be.[78]

The black mark on America's character is most indelible when the decision to use the bomb was both morally suspect and its use proved to be irrelevant to the outcome. It can only be completely erased when it is clear that the decision was motivated by the highest moral standards and turned out to be absolutely necessary.

Many historians dismiss claims that the decision to drop the atomic bomb was primarily driven by "atomic diplomacy," a desire to restructure international power relations after the war. At most they claim that being able to use the atomic bomb for diplomatic leverage in the postwar world was a "bonus." The primary objective, they say, was saving American lives.

One argument for its use holds that because the bomb project cost what was then a very large sum of two billion dollars and was developed secretly without Congress's approval, Roosevelt, Truman, and their advisors feared they risked the wrath of Congress if they didn't use the bomb.[79]

Indeed, some senior officials made such comments, Byrnes and Stimson among them. However, given all of their other concerns over geopolitical issues and the conduct of the war, it is unlikely that cost was the principal motivation. One could make the argument that atomic diplomacy, misguided as it may have been, at least had a purpose that went beyond the personal interests of those who implemented it. The fear of resistance from Congress suggests that some officials were driven by political cowardice at a time when American soldiers were risking—and losing—their lives.

Another explanation for the bomb's use points to the fear that the Japanese war faction would have seen a change in the surrender terms as a sign of weakness and strengthened their resolve to continue fighting. These concerns were shared at one point by the American Joint Chiefs of Staff during the Okinawa campaign, which was unexpectedly lengthy and costly in terms of causalities.[80]

However, the Okinawa campaign was over by June 21, 1945, well before the start of the Potsdam Conference on July 17. By that time, the Joint Chiefs of Staff were again arguing for a change to the surrender terms. Perhaps even more important, Truman was aware that Emperor Hirohito had sent a personal representative to Stalin asking him to intervene with the United States to change the surrender terms.[81] But even this was not enough for Truman to heed Churchill's plea that he change the surrender terms and allow the emperor to continue as the leader of Japan.

One could also infer that atomic diplomacy was a major consideration for Byrnes early in his tenure at the White House based on a comment he made to the physicist Leo Szilard and two other scientists from the Manhattan Project in May of 1945. Szilard had been trying to convince American political leaders that by using the bomb against Japan, "we might start an atomic arms race between America and Russia which might end with the destruction of both countries." According to Szilard, Byrnes replied that "our possessing and demonstrating the bomb would make Russia more manageable in Europe." Szilard's prophetic response was that the "interests of peace might best be served and an arms race avoided by not using the bomb against Japan, keeping it secret, and letting the Russians think that our work on it had not succeeded."[82] None of this proves the argument that atomic diplomacy was the principal motivating factor behind the tactics of delay at Potsdam. But given the evidence, the traditionalists' claims that atomic diplomacy was not the motivating factor seems more like guarding against the "black mark" on America's character than reasonable historical inference.

If the overriding concern for Truman and Byrnes was the saving of American lives and they were merely following policy assumptions from Roosevelt, they would have sought to end the war as soon as the possibility became apparent. They would have changed the surrender demand to allow for the continued presence of the Japanese emperor, especially when they heard of the emperor's entreaties to Stalin. They also would have included the Soviet Union in the ultimatum announced in the Potsdam Declaration.

There were virtually no explicit policy statements during the Roosevelt administration about the use of the bomb. There certainly wasn't a consensus for using the bomb in a surprise attack. On the other hand, there was a very strong set of formal policy decisions making atomic diplomacy the keystone of America's postwar approach to its dealings with the Soviet Union.

In fact, the use of the atomic bomb against Japan was hardly even discussed during Roosevelt's time in office. In a rare exception, in September 1944, Roosevelt met with Vannevar Bush and James Conant, the most senior officials in charge of the Manhattan Project, about whether the bomb "should be dropped on Japan" or "be used only as a threat after a full-scale demonstration." Roosevelt agreed with Bush that the matter "warranted very careful discussion" but felt the question could be "postponed for quite a time" since the United States did not yet have a working bomb.[83] The only explicit statement during that time about the atomic strike against Japan appeared in a secret *aide-mémoire* Roosevelt entered into with Churchill at Hyde Park on September 18, 1944, which stated, "When a bomb is finally available, it might perhaps, after mature consideration, be used against the Japanese, who should be warned that this bombardment will be repeated until they surrender."[84]

But it is unlikely that this agreement had much effect on policymakers in Roosevelt's administration since very few of them even knew it existed. What is perhaps more revealing about Roosevelt's policy regarding the atomic bomb is the agreement he and Churchill signed the previous year in Quebec and the events that led up to it. The Quebec agreement was the result of a major diplomatic effort by Churchill to convince Roosevelt to commit to Anglo-American control of atomic weapons in the postwar period, rather than control by the United States alone.

The initial stages of the Manhattan Project had relied in part on early work done by British scientists and resources from Canada. But in October 1942, Conant concluded that the United States was carrying on the great majority of the work on bomb development. Conant expected a "couple of bombs" to be ready "by the fall of 1944" and moved to scale back the working relationship with Britain.[85]

The official recommendations to do so came from the Top Policy Group, which was responsible for coordinating the scientific aspects of the bomb development with government policy. Its members included Conant; Bush; Army Corps of Engineers General Leslie Groves, who was the director of the Manhattan Project; **Secretary of War Stimson**; and Vice President Henry Wallace. Conant led the argument in favor of severely limiting British and Canadian access to technical details of the bomb development project.

Roosevelt approved the Top Policy Group's recommendation. He did so despite the fact that the report the group sent to Roosevelt stated explicitly that if adopted, the new policy might "slow down" the development of the bomb.[86] U.S. postwar control of the atomic bomb appears to have taken precedence over the need to develop the bomb as quickly as possible.

Conant himself was very clear in that regard: "The major consideration must be that of national security and *postwar strategic significance* [italics in the original]." For the United States to share the technical details of the Manhattan Project "might be the equivalent to joint occupation of a fortress or strategic harbor in perpetuity."[87] In a memo he sent to Roosevelt, Bush was very clear about the risk involved, stating, "We still do not know where we stand in the race with the enemy ... but it is quite possible that Germany is ahead of us and may well be able to produce superbombs sooner than we can."[88]

The British were informed of the new policy on January 13, 1943.[89] In a series of telegrams to Roosevelt, Churchill threatened to divert British research away from other war-related research such as improved radio communications so that Britain could pursue atomic research on its own: "We cannot afford after the war to face the future without this weapon and rely entirely on America, should Russia or some other Power develop it."[90] Roosevelt accepted Churchill's argument and reversed course regarding cooperation with Britain and Canada in May of 1943.

Churchill reiterated his concerns about the postwar importance of the atomic bomb and the danger of delaying its development to Bush and Stimson at a meeting in London in July 1943: "It would never do to have Germany or Russia win the race for something which might be used for international blackmail."[91]

The agreement for renewed cooperation between Britain and the United States was formalized at an August summit conference between the two countries in Quebec. It stated in part that they would never use atomic weapons against each other; they would never use them against a third party without mutual consent; and they would not communicate any information about nuclear weapons without mutual consent.[92]

Nevertheless, damage had already been done. A prominent American scientist working on the Manhattan Project estimated the gap in cooperation caused a delay of the bomb's development of six months to a year or more.[93]

Roosevelt's initial decision to end cooperation with Britain in the development of the bomb should be viewed in the light of the broader context of his thinking about how power would be used in the postwar world and which nations would wield it. As early as August 1941 Roosevelt told Churchill that he rejected the notion that an "effective international police" force could be relied upon to keep the peace; he preferred an Anglo-American police force as a more effective alternative.[94] This was well before the atomic bomb was a factor in his strategic calculations; the Manhattan Project was only authorized in December of that year.

He later broadened the concept of an international police force to include the Soviet Union and China as well as created a proposal that became known as the Four Policemen.[95] Every other nation would be disarmed and, Roosevelt said, the international police force would "build up a reservoir of force so powerful that no aggressor would dare to challenge it." Furthermore, if any nation did challenge the Policemen, that country would be bombed at a rate of a city a day.[96] Roosevelt discussed the concept with then Soviet foreign minister Molotov in 1942. He discussed the idea with Stalin in late 1943 at the Tehran conference.[97]

Once Roosevelt realized the atomic bomb was likely to become a reality, he decided that only two of the policemen, the United States and Great Britain, would have the bomb.[98] Initially, Roosevelt was not averse to the creation of an organization that included all nations at some point after the war as long as its "management" was under the control of the Four Policemen. The proposal eventually led to the creation of the United Nations. The "management" concept was retained as well: With the addition of France and China, the Policemen became the five permanent members of the UN Security Council whose individual veto stops the implementation of actions by the United Nations, including proposed military "peacekeeping" operations.[99]

A couple of months after the Quebec conference, Bush told Conant about a conversation he had with Roosevelt: "The President evidently thought he could join with Churchill in bringing about a US–UK postwar agreement on this subject [the atomic bomb] by which it would be held closely and presumably to control the peace of world."[100]

The notion that the United States could use the atomic bomb to control "the peace of the world" was the underlying assumption that led the Target Committee to declare in early May 1945 that

> psychological factors in the target selection were of great importance. Two aspects of this are (1) obtaining the greatest psychological effect against Japan and (2) making the initial use [of the bomb] sufficiently spectacular for the importance of the weapon to be internationally recognized when publicity on it is released.[101]

Of course, both assumptions could have carried over from the Roosevelt administration: The bomb would be dropped on Japan, and it would be a powerful source of diplomatic leverage over the Soviets after the war. But to emphasize the former without considering more supporting evidence for the latter is not a sound basis for drawing historical inferences. However, another kind of institutional "momentum" had developed during the war. It didn't come from policy decisions by senior members of the Roosevelt or Truman administrations. It developed from the conduct of the war itself. What America was doing in Japan in the spring and summer of 1945 and had already done in Germany would have been almost as hard to justify as Hiroshima and Nagasaki. Indeed, those "conventional" bombing campaigns were almost as important as the Manhattan Project in making the use of the atomic bomb possible.

CHAPTER 2

Conventional Bombing and "Casual Destructiveness"

I
n the five months before Hiroshima, American bombers destroyed almost every Japanese city of any size. By May the destruction was proceeding at such a pace that Secretary of War Stimson and President Truman directed General Hap Arnold, the overall commander of the bombing campaign in Japan, to spare a small list of cities so that suitable targets would be available for the atomic bomb.[1] In mid-July, war planners proposed moving the target criteria downward to include "all urban areas with a population greater than 30,000 people," totaling 180 towns.[2] The United States was well on its way to making Japan, in the words of General Arnold, "a nation without cities."[3]

The first large-scale bombing attacks against the Japanese home islands became possible after the United States captured the Mariana Islands, among them, Saipan. Saipan was close enough to put Japan in range of the newest American bomber, the B-29. The airbases were actually located on Tinian, a small island just off Saipan itself.

The development of Boeing's B-29 Superfortress was a critical factor that made the bombing of Japan possible. It had a longer range than its predecessor, the B-17 Flying Fortress, which was the principal bomber used against Germany. The B 29 could also carry a heavier bomb load and could fly as high as 30,000 feet, well above the range of Japanese fighter planes.

But the flight distance to Japan and back was close to the limit of the new bomber's range. Moreover, the long flights made the technical shortcomings of the B-29 all the more obvious. As the military historian Kenneth Werrell explained,

> Building the B-29 was a complicated undertaking because the bomber used the most powerful engines, the most sophisticated radar, and the most complex fire-control system of the day. Boeing had to work out problems with the aircraft, incorporate numerous modifications, and gear up for mass production, which required the expansion of its facilities and reliance on other manufacturers.[4]

Many of the B-29's shortcomings were overcome through a combination of technical fixes by Boeing and adjustments by air force field commanders. But during the early operations from Tinian in the Mariana Islands, those later improvements were not in evidence. The planes were difficult to maintain, and crews frequently aborted their missions due to mechanical problems: flying missions at high altitude led to freezing equipment, high fuel consumption, and engine problems.[5] The impact of these problems was clear from the results of the first mission launched from Tinian on November 24, 1944. Of the 111 Superfortresses sent on the mission, 17 turned back due to mechanical problems.[6] The weather over Japan also proved to be a major obstacle for the air campaign. In addition to high winds, the Japanese targets were often obscured by clouds, rendering the daylight precision bombing tactics favored by the Army Air Force largely ineffective. These problems, combined with the mechanical issues, frustrated all involved: the crews, their commanders, and, most importantly, the general in charge of the Army Air Force, Hap Arnold.

In early January 1945, Arnold brought in a new commander of the air forces on Tinian, General Curtis LeMay.[7] LeMay was one of the most successful Army Air Force officers. In Germany, he had been given the command of one of the early B-17 bomber groups. In March of 1944, he became the youngest major general in the Army Air Forces. In August of that year, he was put in charge of a group of B-29s based in India that attacked Japanese forces in Southeast Asia and China, plus a few isolated raids against southern Japan. By finding ways to cope with many of the mechanical problems of the planes and improving training, he was able to achieve a very high operational efficiency.[8] Nevertheless, LeMay found himself frustrated by the weather conditions in Japan. "We were still going in too high," he recalled, "still running into to those big jet streams upstairs. And the weather was almost always bad."[9] He decided to risk an entirely new approach that he knew might cost him his command if it failed. Instead, it changed the course of the war.

LeMay decided to send the B-29s in at lower altitudes, allowing them to use less fuel and thus carry a heavier bombload. Because it lessened the strain on the planes' engines, low-altitude flying was also more reliable. In addition, LeMay decided to attack at night guided by radar.

There was considerable risk in this approach. Unlike the Germans, the Japanese had few fighter planes that could operate effectively at night, and although LeMay knew the Japanese had large-caliber guns that could hit bombers at over 20,000 feet, he didn't know if they had smaller antiaircraft weapons that were effective against planes coming in at low altitude. His technical advisors predicted such weapons could easily create losses of 70 percent.[10] Another critical piece of LeMay's new approach was to use incendiary weapons in an attack designed to burn out large urban areas. His first target city was to be Tokyo.

That incendiary weapons would be highly effective against

Japanese cities was anything but a novel idea of LeMay's. By the early 1930s, American airmen had already taken note that Japanese "towns are built largely of wood and paper to resist the devastation of earthquakes and form the greatest aerial targets the world has ever seen. . . . Incendiary projectiles would burn the cities to the ground in short order."[11] The idea gained immediate currency once the United States was at war. Two days after the attack on Pearl Harbor, a senior army planning officer suggested, "Perhaps the best way to offset this initial defeat is to burn Tokyo and Osaka."[12] Firebombing became central to the top air force commanders in Washington. (Across the Atlantic, Winston Churchill was thinking along the same lines when he advocated "burning of Japanese cities by incendiary bombs."[13])

Initially, such plans were predicated on reaching Japan from air bases in Siberia, something the Soviets refused to allow. Burning Japanese cities from the air had to wait until the United States captured the Mariana Islands. By the time it was possible to bomb Japanese cities, the United States had already gained experience in the art of firebombing and other forms of indiscriminate air attacks against civilians in its air war against Germany. The Germans were actually first to use incendiaries during their attack against Warsaw in 1939.[14] The United States and Britain eventually firebombed cities in Germany, most notably Dresden and Hamburg.

The air war in Germany and the developments that led up to it were important precursors to the legitimization of unlimited mayhem. This strategy of attacking civilians rather than military targets was completely at odds with the avowed policy of the United States. The official doctrine was to pursue only "strategic bombing," also known as "precision bombing," against militarily significant targets whose destruction would hamper the ability of the enemy to conduct the war, among them arms factories, oil supplies, and transportation facilities.

The firebombing of Tokyo was different in that it became the prototype for the American strategy of massive, indiscriminate attacks against civilians all across Japan. This was the point at which America left behind any pretext of sparing civilians. Once this line was crossed, it was much easier to imagine the atomic bomb, as shocking as its destructiveness might be, as simply a more efficient way of doing what the bombers had already been doing.

In his book *The Rise of American Airpower: The Creation of Armageddon*, historian Michael Sherry describes how the indiscriminate bombing of civilians came to be seen as morally justified. In 1908, just a few years after the Wright brothers' seminal flight, H.G. Wells published *The War in the Air*, predicting that air warfare would lead to a "destructive scramble" among the great powers that would end with the collapse of Western civilization.[15] But Wells underestimated how long it would take to develop bombers capable of inflicting damage on a large scale. The first widespread use of bombing from the air came during World War I. According to Sherry, by the end of the war "bombs had hit every capital of the warring European powers except Rome."[16]

The intensity of the bombing during the First World War was modest by future standards. The German strategy of attacking civilians in an effort to undermine the British "will to fight" meant that the British sustained the heaviest civilian casualities during that war. By the end of the war, the British had suffered losses of 1,400 killed and 3,400 wounded during the German bombing. The numbers for German civilians were 750 killed and 1,300 injured.[17]

Overall, aerial warfare during World War I had little effect on the outcome of the war itself. But it did much to influence the thinking of both the general public and military planners concerning the future of bombing. While the Germans adopted a strategy of intimidation against British civilians, the British began by concentrating on "precision bombing" directed against Germany's military infrastructure. At the end of the war, the British, too, were preparing to engage in "area bombing" against German cities in response to the attacks against Britain. In the words of British Prime Minister David Lloyd George, "We shall bomb Germany with compound interest!"[18]

Although the war ended before Lloyd George could fulfill his promise, the German admiral Alfred von Tirpitz had already laid out a rationale for justifying it: "Single bombs from flying machines are wrong; they are odious when they hit and kill an old woman. [But] if one could set fire to London in thirty places, then what in a small way is odious would retire before something fine and powerful."[19]

During the two decades after the First World War, the British used air power to subdue recalcitrant colonial subjects in villages in Iraq, Somalia, and Yemen, while the Italians under Mussolini carried out bombing attacks in Ethiopia.[20] There was also considerable speculation during those years that bombers would soon be able to wipe out entire cities with a single strike. One writer imagined how London could be "swept away" by a single bombing attack and "then will the enemy dictate his terms, which will be grasped at like a straw by a drowning man."[21]

Ironically, this vision of total destruction from the air offered a fantasy of freedom from war itself that attracted the hopes of those who had suffered through years of trench warfare. "For them . . . air war remained a doomsday prospect more than a believable danger. They all hoped that nations would shrink from unleashing air war—its horror constituted its virtue by deterring the unthinkable from occurring."[22]

The idea of the unthinkable doomsday being a deterrent to war was still common right up to the eve of World War II. In the 1960s, Harold Macmillan, the former prime minister of Great Britain, recalled: "We thought of air warfare in 1938 rather as people think of nuclear war today."[23]

By the time the United States entered World War II, it had developed a policy that rejected intentional attacks against civilians.

Instead, the American policy called for degrading the enemy's ability to wage war by attacking military infrastructure based on an analysis of the enemy's capabilities and vulnerabilities. Bombings would be in daylight, at high altitude, and with precision bombardment of selected targets.[24]

The United States military believed the B-17 bomber it had developed in the 1930s was perfectly suited to the task. American war planners thought that if fitted with new, accurate bombsights, the planes could fly at altitudes high enough to put them beyond the reach of enemy defenses and reach a carefully chosen target. In daylight, the new bombsights would allow the bombers to destroy critical enemy industrial sites with maximum accuracy and return safely to their home bases.

When the United States entered the war against Germany, the British had already tried to use the same strategy but found it ineffective and suffered heavy losses in the process.[25] Still, they were committed to area bombing against civilians. Their preferred weapon was the incendiary bomb, which they used to devastating effect in Hamburg in the summer of 1944, producing the first massive firestorm of the war. Quoting from contemporary observers, Sherry described the effect on the people of Hamburg:

> The firestorm erupted so rapidly that the population caught in it was trapped. Measures that were sensible in a high-explosive attack—rushing to shelters and basements—were disastrous because the fire drained these quarters of oxygen, asphyxiating inhabitants, then baking the bodies through radiant heat or, if the fire burst through collapsing walls, melting them into "a thick, greasy black mass." . . . The quick-witted could only flee into "a blizzard of red snowflakes" where they often became human torches . . . found "marked with a waxen pallor like dummies in a shop window."[26]

The British rationale for the bombing also presaged what was to become the American rationale for the bombing of Japan. The Royal Air Force "sought victory not by disarming Germans of their sword or disabling the forge that produced it, but by destroying the people manning the forge." This action was not just in order to destroy their morale but, as the RAF's own directive for the battle put it, the "total destruction" of the city in order to "achieve immeasurable results in reducing the industrial capacity of the enemy's war machine."[27]

Sherry suggests that if the results are "immeasurable," there can be no criteria for success or failure for the commanders of an air war as there are for "admirals whose ships sank or generals who lost ground. . . . 'Immeasurable results' . . . were commensurate with almost infinite vengeance."[28] Initially, the British and American commanders ran what were essentially two separate air wars, following their respective strategic preferences. By the end of the war, the two forces had moved toward each other in terms of strategy. The British did develop techniques for better accuracy, although they were employed mostly to allow the destruction of entire cities to be carried out more efficiently.[29]

The American turn toward the British idea of achieving "immeasurable results" may have been motivated in part by a sense of frustration. For one thing, "precision bombing" was not all that precise. American generals considered bombing accuracy in an attack against German ball bearing plants in 1944 to be "good [if] four of the sixteen groups [of bombers] got half or more of their bombs within one thousand feet of the target."[30]

Even when, as in this instance, the attackers were able to destroy the target, their efforts had little effect on the enemy's military capacity: "German stockpiles, redesign of equipment, imports from Sweden, reorganization of production, and the dispersal and protection of the plants muted the much hoped for impact."[31] The change in the American approach to bombing in Europe is best exemplified by the joint British and American firebomb attack against Dresden on the nights of February 13 and 14, 1945. The number of German civilians who died in the attack is estimated to be about 35,000, many of whom had fled other towns that had been destroyed by Allied bombs or the advancing Russian army.

Sherry comments that "the Dresden raids were less the product of conscious callousness than of casual destructiveness." There was no clear rationale for the attack put forward by American planners, although there had been previous plans for terror attacks to destroy German morale and debates as to attacks that would enhance precision bombing or whether they would be "baby killing."[32]

By 1945, the contrast between the American and British approach was a distinction without a difference because the Americans were already relying on inaccurate radar or simply "blind bombing." The fiction of defined targets was only relevant to the extent that it helped American commanders avoid the moral implications that had come with their gradual slide toward terrorizing civilians rather than destroying military targets.[33]

CHAPTER 3

Casual Destructiveness
Comes of Age

By March of 1945 the residents of Tokyo were familiar with B-29 bombing attacks against their city. But they had always come during the day. The one on the 9th of March was different. The raid began shortly before midnight. An eyewitness account described the first bombers to appear as "black silhouettes gliding through the fiery sky" and then shining "golden against the dark roof of heaven or glittering blue, like meteors, in the searchlight beams spraying the vault from horizon to horizon." Then, as the city ignited, they looked "like giant silver moths [attracted] to the towering blaze."[1]

General Curtis LeMay had laid out a careful plan for burning as much of the densely inhabited city as possible. First the bombers laid out a giant X of incendiaries across the city's neighborhoods. For three hours afterward succeeding waves of bombers broadened the fires still further. Many of the incendiaries came down as "a kind of flaming dew that skittered along the roofs, setting fire to everything it splashed and spreading a wash of dancing flames everywhere."[2]

Unlike the sudden annihilation that was to come to victims of Hiroshima and Nagasaki, many people in Tokyo "could see the destruction take place and watch the thing come alive, becoming some living, grotesque organism, ever changing in its shape, dimensions, colors, and directions" before they had to flee.[3] But it was hard to know where to go or what to do. Some "put on the government-prescribed padded hood, which, like bundled babies on the backs of fleeing mothers, often caught fire before the victim knew it."[4] The heat from the advancing fire caused entire blocks of houses to catch fire before the flames themselves reached them. Jumping into a river could leave one boiled alive. And as in Dresden, fire sucked the oxygen from the air.

The attack on Tokyo burned 15.8 square miles at the center of the city. As in Dresden, and in the devastating attack the British mounted against Hamburg, high winds and other factors made ideal conditions for the creation of a particularly intense firestorm. Although the conditions for incendiary attacks were less favorable, the subsequent bombings during March against Nagoya, Osaka, and Kobe did extensive damage. In mid-April a second fire attack against Tokyo destroyed 10.7 square miles. The B-29s returned to Nagoya two more times in May and to Tokyo twice more. At Stimson's urging, Roosevelt had decided to spare Japan's ancient capital and fourth largest city Kyoto. By mid-June, the air campaign against six of the seven largest Japanese cities had ended.[5]

The targets often seemed to have been chosen because they were "operationally easy rather than strategically vital." The town of Oita with sixty thousand refugees had no major industry, although it did have a naval air depot—which was not attacked. Instead, a mid-July attack using 790 tons of incendiaries destroyed "banks, a soya sauce factory, two schools, a Presbyterian church."[6]

Similar attacks were launched against the cities of Aomori, Hachioji, Ube, and Hamamatsu, all of which had little military significance, and to the extent there were any military targets, they seemed to have been ignored. Hamamatsu is particularly noteworthy. LeMay called it "the garbage-can target" where bomber crews dumped unused munitions they had not been able to use against their assigned targets.[7]

If one measures "results" simply in terms of the amount of destruction the firebombing campaign caused, one would consider it very successful. The attacks destroyed 99.5 percent of the acreage of the city of Toyama, for example. Overall, the United States' firebombing destroyed an estimated 180 square miles of sixty-seven cities, killed more than 300,000 people, and injured an additional 400,000.[8]

In justifying these attacks, U.S. airmen in Japan performed the same linguistic sleight of hand as their colleagues in Europe. They did so even among themselves. An internal report maintained, "these operations were not conceived as terror raids against the civilian population." Their purpose "was *not* to bomb indiscriminately civilian populations. The object was to destroy the *industrial and strategic targets* [italics in the original] concentrated in the urban areas."[9]

Within days of the Tokyo firebombing, officials in Washington were feeling pressure from the press that "blanket incendiary attacks upon cities" implied a move away from precision bombing. The chief of staff to the Twentieth Bomber Command held a press conference in Washington in an attempt to invoke the idea behind precision bombing, claiming that the bombings were "the most economical method of destroying the small industries in these areas."[10]

A few months later, an article in the *New Yorker* by St. Clair McKelway, the public relations officer for the Twenty-First Bomber Command in the Mariana Islands, claimed, "It was pin-point, incendiary bombing from a low level, designed not simply to start fires or destroy a single factory but to start one great conflagration whose fury would double and redouble the destructive force of the bombs."[11] This was the "something fine and powerful" Alfred von Tirpitz had looked forward to over two decades earlier.

Later that summer, military planners had the air force drop leaflets over Japanese cities warning the inhabitants in advance of a bombing attack and urging them to surrender. Air force officials believed the warnings helped "lessen the stigma attached to area bombing."[12]

The members of the Interim Committee employed similar language in their planning for the use of the atomic bomb. At a May 31, 1945, meeting they agreed "we could not concentrate on a civilian area" while also declaring that "the most desirable target would be a vital war plant . . . closely surrounded by workers' houses." They also concluded "that we could not give the Japanese any warning," because "we should seek to make a profound psychological impression on as many inhabitants as possible."[13]

The shift from self-deception to an outright lie reached its completion with Truman's August 9 announcement of the bombing of Hiroshima. The announcement took advantage of the presence of a nearby military headquarters and described Hiroshima as a "military base" while omitting the fact that it was a city of 300,000 people:

> The world will note that the first atomic bomb was dropped on Hiroshima, a military base. That was because we wished in this first attack to avoid, insofar as possible, the killing of civilians. But that attack is only a warning of things to come. If Japan does not surrender, bombs will have to be dropped on her war industries and, unfortunately, thousands of civilian lives will be lost. I urge Japanese civilians to leave industrial cities immediately, and save themselves from destruction.[14]

The language of Truman's announcement is consistent with the language American military and civilian leaders used to legitimate the bombing of civilians throughout the war. It is the language of "casual destructiveness" used to justify firebombing the civilians of both Japan and Germany. That language made atomic bombing easier to accept for the American public and those whose task it was to carry out the raids.

Public support for the atomic bombings immediately after the end of the war was overwhelming. Polls showed that 85 percent approved of the bombings.[15] Such a reaction was understandable. After four years of war, almost 300,000 American soldiers had been killed in combat, with over two-thirds of those deaths occurring in 1944 and the first half of 1945.[16] It is not surprising, then, that the press assumed the bombings were justified.

That unanimity of support did not last. As early as September 1945, several prominent religious figures questioned the atomic bombings. The editor of the *Catholic World* declared it would call the use of the bomb "a crime were it not that the word 'crime' implies sin and sin requires consciousness of guilt." The bombing "was in defiance of every sentiment and every conviction upon which our civilization is based." The Protestant *Christian Century* said the atomic bombing "has placed our nation in an indefensible moral position."[17]

Some secular sources were even more insistent in their criticism. David Lawrence, a political conservative and owner of the *United States News*—soon to be renamed the *U.S. News and World Report*—compared the use of the atomic bomb to the "quick and instantaneous . . . lethal chambers of Buchenwald" and noted that "spokesmen for our Air Forces tell us [the war] could have been readily won without the atomic bomb."[18]

Although these initial criticisms were by well-known intellectuals, they were not read by the general public. In 1946, criticism started coming from more widely read sources. A commentary in the *Saturday Review of Literature* asked, "Can it be that we were more anxious to prevent Russia from establishing a claim . . . against Japan than we were to think through the implications of unleashing atomic warfare?"[19]

On August 31, 1946, the *New Yorker* devoted an entire issue to John Hersey's *Hiroshima*, an intensely moving account of the human suffering caused by the bomb. Many newspapers reprinted the entire thirty-thousand-word account. In the fall, the Book of the

Month Club sent hundreds of thousands of free copies to its members. Hersey's book told the stories of six survivors of the atomic bombing of Hiroshima with a sense of immediacy of experience not easily found elsewhere:

> Mr. Tanimoto found about twenty men and women on the sandspit. He drove the boat onto the bank and urged them to get aboard. They did not move and he realized that they were too weak to lift themselves. He reached down and took a woman by the hands, but her skin slipped off in huge, glove-like pieces. He was so sickened by this that he had to sit down for a moment. . . . He had to keep consciously repeating to himself, "These are human beings."[20]

The rising level of criticism alarmed prominent chemist James Conant, the president of Harvard University and administrator of the Manhattan Project. He felt it was necessary to discredit the rising criticism and approached the then former Secretary of War Henry Stimson to write a rebuttal to the critics.

The elderly Stimson was in poor health and turned over much of the work to a ghostwriter, whose text was then heavily edited by Conant. The essay was published in the February 1947 issue of *Harper's Magazine*.[21]

Joseph Grew, the former acting Secretary of State, wrote a letter criticizing the *Harper's* piece for claiming there was no alternative to using the atomic bomb when both he and Stimson had been advising the president to include reassurances that Japan could keep its emperor system. Grew wrote:

> I and a good many others will always feel that had the President issued as far as May 1945, the . . . statement that the Japanese dynasty could be retained . . . the atom bomb might never have had to be used at all.[22]

Stimson's obfuscation over the question of the surrender terms was not the only part of the picture he left hidden from view. His characterization of the ensuing invasion that he claimed would have been unavoidable without the use of the atomic bomb was also misleading. The invasion was scheduled to start on November 1 and, he claimed, "might be expected to cost over a million" dead and wounded American soldiers.[23]

There is no evidence of that number of American casualties in any estimate by the military leaders planning the invasion. But the obfuscation was taken up by others besides Stimson. According to a research paper at the CIA's Center for the Study of Intelligence, the estimate given to Truman on June 18, 1945, by the Joint War Plans Committee in charge of planning the invasion was 220,000. The paper describes how in 1953 Truman received a request from a historian for information about the casualty estimates for the invasion given to him by Chief of Staff George Marshall. Truman's initial reply was that Marshall told him "one quarter of a million would be the minimum" number of dead and wounded. Truman's staff altered the reply before it was sent so that it read "at a minimum one quarter of a million casualties and might cost as much as a million." The phrase "as much as a million" was added in order to make the reply consistent with Stimson's article in *Harper's*.[24]

It is also quite possible that the Kyushu invasion might never have happened. By the time of the June 18 meeting, intelligence information had arrived indicating the Japanese were rapidly increasing the number of troops on Kyushu, the island on the Japanese homeland the Americans were planning as the site of their planned invasion.

By August, the number of Japanese troops on Kyushu had grown to twice the number used to plan the invasion and three times the number of troops in the part of the island where the invasion was to take place. The Joint Chiefs were ready to consider choosing an alternate invasion site or abandoning the invasion plan altogether and relying on a naval blockade and continued bombing instead. A meeting to consider such options was being planned for the same day the bombing of Hiroshima occurred. As Douglas MacEachin notes in a retrospective study published by the Central Intelligence Agency, *"If the atomic bomb had not been ready and used when it was, this JCS meeting would have been held [italics in the original]."*[25]

Of course, the military leaders could only think in terms of what their own forces could accomplish. They couldn't take into account what the Soviets might do. But the Soviets almost certainly would have been anxious to "get in on the kill" if the United States had chosen to invade Japan or beat it into submission with a blockade and continued bombing. Either option would have taken more time—time enough to allow Stalin ample opportunity to seize territory in northern Japan.

That was precisely what Truman was trying to avoid. It was also what the war party in the Japanese government was trying to avoid. The Japanese army leaders knew they could not simultaneously fight a Russian invasion from the north and an American invasion from the south. They decided to place all their bets on stopping the American invasion by massing their troops at Kyushu, even though doing so weakened their defenses against a possible Soviet attack.

Avoiding a Soviet invasion was also the goal of the peace party, whose members were secretly petitioning Stalin to intervene with the Americans to change the surrender terms" in favor of retaining the emperor. Meanwhile, the war party had its own secret plan for approaching Stalin. They hoped to entice the Soviets to remain neutral by offering them almost all of the territory Japan had acquired as a result of the Russo–Japanese War in 1905 as well as territory it had wrested from China a decade earlier.[26]

Keeping the Russians out of Japan seems to have been the one thing everybody agreed upon. Everyone except, of course, the Russians themselves.

CHAPTER 4

Postwar Atomic Diplomacy

The comments in the popular press of the time show that by the summer of 1946 there was at least a hint in the air that atomic diplomacy may have played a role in the use of the atomic bomb in Japan. In fact, James F. Byrnes, secretary of state, tried his hand at atomic diplomacy several months earlier, in September 1945. At that time Byrnes attended the London Council of Foreign Ministers, where he met with his British and Soviet counterparts, Ernest Bevin and Vyacheslav Molotov, as well as representatives from France and China.

The former ambassador to the Soviet Union, Joseph Davies, tried to warn Byrnes against attempting to use the atomic bomb for diplomatic advantage. In a conversation they had at Potsdam, Davies explained that Byrnes's reliance on the atomic bomb was dangerously misplaced, that politically it was "full of unknown and dangerous psychological explosive power." He warned that the Soviets would view any attempt to exploit an Anglo-American atomic monopoly as a hostile act. The Russians "would naturally see it as deliberately throwing them out on the junk heap after they had been 'used' to defeat Hitler." His entreaties had little effect.[1]

The meeting in London was Byrnes's first opportunity to act independently as secretary of state without Truman's presence. Truman had given him significant leeway in engaging with foreign officials without him. "Use your best judgment and I am sure that thing[s] will come out all right," Truman told him.[2]

Yet, as Byrnes well knew, this was likely to be a difficult and delicate encounter with the Soviets. The Council of Foreign Ministers had been established at Potsdam as the body that would attempt to address issues that the two sides were not able to resolve at Potsdam. Now that the war was over, the Soviets were still firmly implanted in Eastern Europe and had new grievances over the way they were treated in the Far East.

Byrnes understood that he could not issue explicit threats about the bomb. Rather, he thought it would be an invisible yet powerful presence at the conference that would cause the Soviets to be far more circumspect in their dealings with the United States and Britain. Stimson privately took note of Byrnes's dilemma: "[His] mind is full of his problems with the coming meeting of the foreign ministers and he looks to have the presence of the bomb in his pocket, so to speak, as a great weapon to get through the thing he has."[3]

Byrnes had a rude awakening after a day of unproductive negotiations with Molotov on September 13, the second day of the conference. Ironically, the image Molotov used was the same as the one Stimson had invoked a few days earlier. Molotov asked Byrnes if he had "an atomic bomb 'in his side pocket.'" Byrnes responded: "'You don't know Southerners. We carry our artillery in our hip pocket. If you don't cut out all this stalling and let us get down to work, I'm going to pull an atomic bomb out of my hip pocket and let you have it.'"[4]

The Soviets continued to pursue their own version of atomic diplomacy several other times during the conference. One instance came at a cocktail party where Molotov, appearing slightly inebriated, raised a toast to the atomic bomb and said, "We've got it," before other members of the Soviet delegation maneuvered him out of the room. But Byrnes didn't believe the Russians had the bomb. Instead, he saw the Russians' behavior as a blustering attempt to hide their inferiority.[5]

The negotiations in London quickly devolved into a stalemate. Molotov resisted demands by the United States and Britain that the Soviets allow the Balkan states, including Romania (then known in English-speaking countries as Rumania) and Bulgaria, to conform to political standards called for by the agreement reached at Yalta. The agreement called for "free and unfettered elections" and "governments truly representative of 'all democratic elements.'" Byrnes interpreted those provisions to mean that Western election observers and journalists would have sufficient access in those countries to ensure that elections met those standards.[6]

These demands appeared to the Soviets as an attempt to renege on what was agreed to at Yalta—that after the war they would have spheres of influence over the Balkan countries along the Soviet border. Since obtaining such spheres of influence along its western borders had been a Russian geopolitical goal that long predated the Bolshevist Revolution, the Soviets considered the Anglo-American demands to be a threat to Russian security. Molotov pointed to Western control of Greece and Italy as examples of a double standard on the part of the British and the Americans. He also cited America's sole control over Japan. Byrnes admitted to a member of the American delegation, "We were going off in a unilateral way [in Japan] as the Russians were going off in the Balkans."[7]

The Russians, however, were not being as unilateral in the Balkans as Byrnes's comments would suggest. During the month before the opening of the conference, Byrnes had openly intervened in Bulgarian politics. On August 13, four days after the atomic bombing of Nagasaki, he ignored the Soviet commander in Bulgaria, who was the recognized authority under the armistice terms, and sent an open letter to the Bulgarian prime minister demanding that upcoming elections be delayed. The American representative in the Balkans described the action as a "major diplomatic effort" in support of the pro-Western opposition in the country.[8]

Stalin, who up to that point had not openly intervened in

Bulgaria, quickly moved to support the pro-Soviet faction then in power by granting it diplomatic recognition. A commentator in the *New York Times* remarked that "the Bulgarian situation . . . is likely to produce an early deadlock in the work of the new Council of Foreign Ministers."[9]

The diplomatic correspondent for the *London Times* expanded on the same theme:

> What must chiefly be regretted is that a new complication is added to Allied relations. The Soviet Government has already recognized the Bulgarian Government and has sent an Ambassador to Sofia. . . . A peace treaty can be made only with a recognized Government—and London and Washington appear to be committed not to recognize the Bulgarian Government. A deadlock appears inevitable.[10]

The conflict over Bulgaria led to a public display of atomic diplomacy while the foreign ministers were still meeting. Mass street demonstrations in Bulgaria were accompanied by chants of "We don't fear the atomic bomb!"[11]

The London meeting of the Council of Foreign Ministers ended on October 12 without having reached any agreements. Byrnes felt the failure in London as a personal blow; he had staked much of his reputation as a skilled international negotiator and personal diplomacy expert on his success in London. As one member of the American delegation at London observed, Byrnes was "extremely nervous . . . tired out and exhausted, and facing this failure of his first mission on his own was getting under his skin."[12]

Byrnes, it is fair to say, was a victim of his own naivete when it came to diplomatic matters. Shortly before setting out for London, Byrnes claimed he knew how to deal with the Russians. "It's just like the U.S. Senate. You build a post office in their state and they'll build a post office in our state."[13] But shortly after the conference, he said, "The Russians are stubborn, obstinate, and they don't scare."[14]

He was also trapped by the changing political climate back home. The secrecy that had surrounded diplomatic efforts during the war, such as those at Yalta and Potsdam, was no longer in effect once the war was over. Political conservatives in the House and the Senate were becoming increasingly restive about possible compromises with the Soviet Union.

While he was still in London, Byrnes got a taste of what was soon to become a highly volatile issue in American politics. He was no doubt aware that with the end of the war, Congress, including its Republican members, would have influence on the conduct of foreign affairs. In recognition of that fact, and perhaps due to his confidence that his use of atomic diplomacy would ensure his success, he invited a prominent Republican Party spokesman, John Foster Dulles, to accompany him to London.

Matters took a difficult turn once Molotov invoked atomic diplomacy in reverse. Realizing that the atomic bomb might actually be a barrier to reaching an accommodation with the Soviet Union, Byrnes told Dulles: "We have pushed these babies [the Russians] as far as they will go and I think that we better start thinking about compromise." Dulles would have none of it and warned Byrnes that he would publicly denounce any attempt at compromise in London as a violation of "principle and morality" on par with the appeasement of Hitler before the war.[15]

Nonetheless, Byrnes still believed it was possible to forge a good working relationship with the Soviet Union. Molotov seemed to him to be the real obstacle. Byrnes's personal secretary, Walter Brown, wrote in his journal that Byrnes "saw no hope of stopping M[olotov] except by appealing to Stalin. He thinks Stalin wants peace."[16]

Truman also had a somewhat favorable view of the Soviet leader: "I can deal with Stalin." This sentiment, also shared by some in the

State Department, was probably a result of the successful personal diplomacy Roosevelt had been able to employ with Stalin at Yalta.[17]

Fortunately for Byrnes and Truman, press coverage of U.S. administration policy regarding the Soviet Union was still mostly favorable. Although there were frequent mentions of a "two bloc world"[18] emerging from the meeting in London, Molotov was receiving most of the blame for the failure of the conference. There was still an opportunity for Byrnes to redeem his reputation as a diplomat. He pinned his hopes on a personal meeting with Stalin in Moscow.

After the London Council of Foreign Ministers, Byrnes came to view the bomb as a threat hardening Soviet resistance to diplomatic solutions concerning geopolitical issues such as those in the Balkans and the Far East. Before Byrnes left for Moscow, former American ambassador to the Soviet Union W. Averell Harriman helped clarify for him "the real effect of the atomic bomb on [the] Soviet attitude." Harriman explained that Germany's defeat and the Red Army's presence in the nations along Russia's western border gave the Soviet leadership a sense of security they hadn't had before. But the atomic bomb undermined that sense of security and contributed to their defensive and hostile responses to the American diplomatic initiatives. The reaction to the bomb, he told Byrnes, "Partially explains Molotov's aggressiveness in London."[19]

Accompanied by British Foreign Minister Ernest Bevin, Byrnes began negotiations with Molotov in Moscow. Byrnes managed to get Molotov to agree to a general framework for the international control of atomic energy. He hoped this framework would be the basis of negotiations at the General Meeting of the United Nations in June 1946, where they aimed to establish a United Nations commission for the control of atomic energy. He also made a number of compromises regarding the governance of the Eastern European countries under Soviet control.[20]

Both moves on Byrnes's part ran afoul of domestic politics in the U.S. that were becoming increasingly anti-Soviet in tone. To be sure, there were still important voices of moderation in the Truman administration urging accommodation with the Soviets, among them Henry Stimson; Secretary of Commerce and former Vice President under Roosevelt Henry Wallace; Undersecretary of State Dean Acheson; and Vannevar Bush.

But the advocates of a strong anti-Soviet stance included Truman's Chief of Staff Admiral William Leahy; Secretary of the Navy James Forrestal; and Secretary of the Treasury Frederick Vinson. Making matters more difficult for Truman was the growing influence of political figures outside of his administration. These included John Foster Dulles, Senator Arthur Vandenberg of Michigan, Tom Connally of Texas, and Scott Lucas of Illinois. Leslie Groves, the director of the Manhattan Project, also became a key figure in the development of America's confrontational approach to its postwar relationship with the Soviet Union despite the fact that he had no direct role at the White House and as a military officer was obligated to refrain from political advocacy. Groves was to become a key figure in the development of America's confrontational approach to its postwar relationship with the Soviet Union.[21]

As far as Truman was concerned, Byrnes had overstepped the considerable latitude Truman had allowed him in the conduct of foreign affairs by agreeing to share information about atomic energy with the Soviets. The president also took issue with the concessions Byrnes had granted the Soviets regarding the Balkans.

These agreements left Truman vulnerable to the hard-liners, especially Senator Vandenberg and his allies in Congress. Moreover, whether out of conviction or political necessity, Truman himself was taking an increasingly hard-line stance. Byrnes returned from Moscow a few days after Christmas 1945, and on January 6, Truman told Byrnes the Moscow agreements were "unreal" and "no more than a general promise" from the Soviets. Byrnes, Truman complained, "had taken it upon himself to move the foreign policy of the United States in a direction to which he could not, and would not, agree." "I'm tired of babying the Soviets," Truman said.[22]

What Truman failed to consider was that drawing a "hard line" against a potential enemy does not make that potential enemy more malleable, especially when the country in question is a major power like the Soviet Union. In this instance, Truman's new policy turned out to be a major step toward the Cold War.

CHAPTER 5

The Atomic "Secret"

The fear that the Soviet Union would ferret out America's "atomic secret" became a major political issue, one that made for spectacular headlines in the press. Domestic atomic politics in the United States were already beginning their ascent as early as October 1945, while Byrnes was still at the London Council of Foreign Ministers meeting. Yet the biggest secret was that there was no secret.

Truman and other decision-makers in his administration well understood that the knowledge needed to build an atomic bomb fell into three basic categories. Truman defined those categories in a speech he gave in early October 1945. The first was the "scientific knowledge that resulted in the atomic bomb," which was "worldwide knowledge already." The second was the engineering knowledge necessary to build a bomb. That knowledge was something other countries would be able to acquire in the reasonably near future, especially Great Britain. Truman's third category was that only America possessed the "combination of industrial capacity and resources necessary to produce the bomb."[1]

Stimson and Bush had earlier pointed out that none of these three categories presented unsurmountable obstacles that other nations would be unable to overcome in the fairly near future. They suggested the United States might be able to avoid an arms race by sharing technical information with other nations. Truman rejected their suggestions. Nations that wished to "catch up" to the United States, he said, would "have to do it on their own hook, just as we did."[2]

Shortly after delivering the speech, an old friend of Truman's from Missouri visited the president at the White House. Referring to the speech about atomic secrecy, the friend asked, "Then, Mister President, what it amounts to is this. That the armaments race is on, is that right?" The guest recorded that Truman agreed with that assessment "but added that we would stay ahead" and that "his attitude appeared . . . to be that of a man who had made up his mind and was supremely confident of the correctness of the decision which he had made."[3]

Truman's newfound confidence in the United States' ability to maintain its hold over the atomic bomb came from assertions by General Groves. A few days before his October speech, Truman sent a close friend and speechwriter to talk to Groves and relay to him a summary of the issues related to nuclear security. Groves was adamantly opposed to cooperation with the Soviets or any other nation regarding the atomic bomb. The general asserted that "we can always be ahead" and that the Russians would need ten to twenty years to build a bomb.[4]

Grove's assessment became widely accepted in the Truman administration. Ever eager to find a way to leverage the power of the bomb, Byrnes enthusiastically embraced the notion that the United States would enjoy a long-term atomic monopoly. He said he "bowed to [the scientists] in their ability to develop the bomb but on the question of giving information to others he thought the scientists were no better informed than he was on the construction of the bomb." Byrnes dismissed the assessment from three prime contractors of the Manhattan Project that Russians could build a bomb within five years. "General Groves knew more about the problem than any of the people from Dupont, Union Carbide or

Eastman [Kodak]."[5]

Ultimately, Truman and many others in his administration relied on Groves's assurances that the atomic secret could remain safely in America's grasp: "This common belief in a prolonged monopoly safeguarded by secrecy was one of the greatest miscalculations of the cold war [sic]" and was, at least in part, a product of "wishful thinking."[6]

Groves's confident assertions concerning America's long-term monopoly over atomic weaponry were based on his quixotic, and at times even tragicomic, attempt to exert worldwide control over the supply of uranium and other fissionable material.

When Groves became head of the Manhattan Project in 1942, he was quick to note that the virtually unprecedented level of secrecy he was working under afforded him the opportunity to involve himself well beyond overseeing the development of the bomb itself. He decided to become involved in "matters of extremely high-level policy, including international relations" aimed at rendering the Russians unable to build an atomic bomb due to the United States' "preclusive" control over the world's uranium.[7] To that end, in 1943, he started a top-secret project under his personal direction, code-named the Murray Hill Area, to locate and purchase uranium ore wherever it was to be found. The project was sanctioned by Roosevelt and Secretary of War Stimson, and it was so secret that the funds for the project were directed through Groves's personal bank account to deter spies and, as he noted in his memoirs, to keep the project going in case of a "change of heart on the part of Congress."[8]

One of Groves's earliest uranium acquisitions came through Edgar Sengier, a Belgian citizen who was an official with a mining consortium that controlled the world's largest deposit of uranium ore in the Belgian Congo. Sengier arrived in New York in 1940, just before Germany took over the Belgian Congo, with a substantial shipment of uranium ore. Groves promptly bought the ore and assumed Sengier would help him negotiate with the Belgian government-in-exile for control of the Congolese mines after the war.

The fact that the primary known use of uranium up to that time was the manufacture of glass and ceramics made such negotiations relatively simple undertakings for the Americans. However, Groves's associates were quite capable of making the job much harder than it might have been otherwise. One such member was an American major named H. S. Traynor, who was introduced to the Belgians as a civilian. On the second day of negotiations, Traynor forgot his role and appeared wearing his military uniform. The surprise presence of an American military officer at the meeting caused the Belgians to suddenly raise the price of the uranium, but Traynor resolved the price dispute when he quietly suggested to Sengier—there as a "neutral 'adviser'" for the Belgians—that his negotiations should reflect what could happen if his Belgian colleagues became aware of his relationship with the United States and decided to charge him with treason.[9]

The Murray Hill Area Project began negotiations with seven other nations for control of uranium deposits, only to be informed by Manhattan Project scientists that they had discovered that another radioactive element, thorium, could also be used to build an atomic bomb. Thorium is about ten times more common than uranium. Undeterred, Groves expanded his efforts.to include American control over thorium deposits.[10]

Of course, after Hiroshima it became much more difficult to purchase preclusive access to fissionable materials from other nations. And prospecting for uranium on U.S. soil no doubt became of far greater interest than it had been when it was primarily used in the manufacture of specialty glass.

The Russians were also anxious to find sources of high-quality uranium well before the end of the war. Both they and Groves knew about uranium mines in Czechoslovakia. Groves was fairly certain that the Czech sources did not produce uranium of high enough quality to be readily used for atomic weapons, although as it turned out, the Soviets were able to exploit them. What Groves did not know was that rich deposits of uranium would soon be found in the Soviet zone of occupied Germany, just across the Czech border. These deposits became the Soviet Union's principal source of uranium, although other significant deposits were found within the Soviet Union by the early 1950s.[11]

Groves also involved himself in domestic matters of "extremely high-level policy," as well as international ones. Congress was beginning to consider legislation that would regulate control over atomic energy. In October of 1945, there were two rival bills before Congress. The first, known as the May–Johnson Bill, would have allowed the military continued control over atomic energy by creating a commission dominated by members of the armed forces. A second bill, known as the McMahon Bill, proposed transferring control over atomic energy from the military to an atomic energy commission composed of civilians. Groves adamantly supported the May–Johnson Bill. He opposed the McMahon Bill. Not only would the McMahon Bill end his command over atomic energy; it was also intended to facilitate international control of atomic weapons. Groves wrote to Byrnes that "it would be an easier task to outlaw war itself" than to establish an effective means of control over atomic weapons.[12]

At first Truman seemed to back Groves's position in support of the May-Johnson Bill and supported Groves's refusal to testify in Senate hearings for the McMahon Bill, citing the need for secrecy. Yet just a few weeks before, Truman had strongly implied there was no real secret to building an atomic bomb.

By January, Truman had changed his stance and supported the McMahon Bill.

His shift was probably influenced by the surprising support for the McMahon Bill by some political conservatives in the Senate, including Senators Scott Lucas and Arthur Vandenberg. Truman may have also been angered by insubordination on the part of Groves and Secretary of War Patterson in their unremitting opposition to civilian control, which they expressed publicly. Groves campaigned for the passage of the May–Johnson Bill in public speeches, a violation of his oath as a military officer. The *New York Times* quoted his bellicose testimony before Congress: "With atomic weapons a nation must be ready to strike the first blow if needed. The first blow or series of blows may be the last."[13]

In a diary entry from the time, Secretary of Commerce Henry Wallace wrote:

> After noting the way in which the Army has spread rumors . . . I am inclined to think they will knife anybody who, directly or indirectly, fights the legislation which they are pushing. . . . The war psychology has gotten into their blood and the ends justify the means. I am expecting them to circulate the most absurd stories.[14]

That is precisely what they did. They circulated absurd stories about spies who were supposedly in hot pursuit of the nonexistent "atomic secret."

Groves had been aware of Soviet espionage directed at the Manhattan Project as early as 1942. He and Secretary of War Stimson had kept both Roosevelt and Truman informed of those efforts. All of them were aware that there was little of value that the Soviets could steal. For that reason, they were not greatly concerned about the presence of Soviet spies, although they did keep track of them. The army's history of its counterintelligence includes hidden microphones, cameras, and other spy equipment as well as agents taking undercover jobs as "electricians, painters, exterminators, contractors, gamblers, etc." According to the army, one agent took a job as a hotel bellhop and proved so able at the position that he was soon promoted to bell captain.[15]

Groves's behavior throughout the controversy over atomic spies was consistent with what a friend of Wallace, a Manhattan Project contractor, told him: "Groves is slightly pathological."[16]

Groves was eager to take advantage of a widespread belief among the public and members of the Senate Committee on Atomic Energy, as well as other government officials who should have known better, that there was an "atomic secret." As Vannevar Bush scathingly put it, it was as if this putative secret were "written perhaps on a single sheet of paper, some sort of magic formula. If we guarded this, we alone could have atomic bombs indefinitely."[17]

In early February 1946, the journalist Drew Pearson told his radio listeners that a Soviet espionage group had been uncovered in Canada. A week later the Canadian Prime Minister, Mackenzie King, announced that twenty-two suspects had been arrested. King also said the premature disclosure by Pearson had forced the Canadian police to arrest the suspects before the investigation was complete. King believed that the disclosure was the result of a "certain kind of politics . . . played by a certain type of man" who wanted to "pave the way" for the spy story "being continued into the U.S."[18]

General Leslie Groves was that "certain type of man." No record exists of Drew Pearson's source concerning the Canadian spy ring, but Groves is known to be Washington columnist Frank McNaughton's "confidential source" for his story, which broke the same day King announced the arrests in Canada. McNaughton wrote about another spy ring operating in the United States that had not been broken up because of the "arguments of state department men—who [the source] will not name that to do so would upset our relations with Russia."[19]

The startling revelations of Soviet spies in the context of popular belief in the existence of an "atomic secret" led to what Gregg Herken described in his book, *The Winning Weapon: The Atomic Bomb in the Cold War, 1945–1950*, as "near-hysteria" over Russian spies. The resulting furor undermined support among the public and in Congress for civilian control through an atomic energy commission.

Groves helped close off further debate about civilian control of atomic energy with a letter he sent to the conservative Republican senator Bourke Hickenlooper, who read the letter on the Senate floor. The senator spoke of the "Pilgrim fathers, who went to church with their muskets loaded" before repeating Groves's inaccurate claims that a British physicist who had been recently arrested and charged with spying knew the secrets of America's atomic bomb "know-how."[20]

Congress eventually passed a version of the McMahon Bill that included an amendment, proposed by Senator Vandenberg, that created a board of military officers who could block the decisions of the civilian commissioners and force them to the president's desk for review.[21]

"It was very clear to me," Wallace wrote in his diary, "that Groves could use the plea of protecting against Russian spies to do anything he wants to. . . . A fellow like Groves, using the Russian phobia as a screen, can, if the military is given the power it desires, go to almost any excess."[22]

Wallace's observation was a prescient one. The struggle for international cooperation to avoid a nuclear arms race was just beginning and Groves played an important role in shaping the outcome.

CHAPTER 6

In Search of International Control

The myth of the "atomic secret" paired neatly with a rapidly developing hard-line stance toward the Soviet Union, which aimed at undermining attempts to establish international control of atomic weapons through the United Nations

In January of 1946, Secretary of State Byrnes appointed the former director of the Tennessee Valley Authority, David Lilienthal, to the newly created Secretary of State's Committee on Atomic Energy to focus on its international control. The committee was chaired by Dean Acheson, the assistant secretary of state.

Lilienthal noted in his journal that he suspected there was no substance to the notion of an atomic secret and that "since it is in the Army's hands (or, literally, Gen. Groves'), to deny access to the facts that would prove or disprove this vital thesis, there has been no way to examine the very foundation of our policies in the international field."[1]

Lilienthal's concerns were the subject of an unlikely exchange of letters between the pacifist A. J. Muste and John Foster Dulles in the summer of 1945. Muste wrote: "So long as we have our tremendous military establishment and the atomic bomb, they determine our relations . . . and our methods." He believed the Soviet Union's attitude toward the United States was largely a consequence of their "fear of us and our atomic bombs."[2]

Dulles responded: "Resort by Soviet leaders to measures of forceful coercion" against their own people had been "characteristic for nearly 30 years . . . long preceding the atomic bomb . . . and they are attempting in foreign affairs to do precisely what they have been doing at home for nearly 30 years."[3]

Muste replied to Dulles with the rejoinder: "You speak of 'the secrecy which surrounds what is going on within the Soviet Union.' What but secrecy surrounds the atomic bomb stockpile? Are we not asking Russia to raise the 'iron curtain' at the same time that we keep the atomic curtain down tight?"[4]

The Secretary of State's Committee on Atomic Energy developed a proposal for establishing international control of atomic energy called the Acheson–Lilienthal Report, which was to be the basis of negotiations at a meeting of the United Nations in June 1946. The report called for the establishment of an international authority to control the mining, refining, and military use of uranium and other fissionable material.

However, the man Byrnes appointed to head the American delegation on atomic energy control to the United Nations rewrote most of the proposal, changing it in such a way that the likelihood of it being adopted was virtually nil. That man was Bernard Baruch, a well-known seventy-five-year-old financier and philanthropist. Baruch was popular with the public and the press, and as Herken put it, "during two world wars" he had "established a largely self-promoted reputation as a close confidant of several American presidents."[5]

Acheson and several of his colleagues were not at all pleased with his appointment to head the delegation. Acheson wrote in his journal that he was "quite sick" over the appointment, and what was needed was someone who was "not vain, and who the Russians would feel isn't out simply to put them in a hole, not really caring about international cooperation. Baruch has none of these qualifications."[6]

Baruch then appointed his "team" for the delegation. They consisted largely of businessmen, several of whom had worked with Baruch on boards that coordinated military production during the First and Second World Wars, as well as a mining engineer who was also a personal friend. Vannevar Bush, one of the supporters of the Acheson–Lilienthal Report, noted the absence of scientists in the group and called them "Wall Streeters." Lilienthal commented that "it is the old crowd" and described one member as "that familiar bull in the china closet."[7]

Baruch did invite some of the drafters of the Acheson–Lilienthal Report to join his delegation, but none of them believed Baruch would really listen to them. Their suspicion was well founded. Baruch later told Lilienthal that he "'could smell his way through' the problems of international control without scientific or technical advice"; and he told Bush, "I concluded that I would drop the scientists because ... I knew all I wanted to know. It went boom and it killed millions of people and I thought it was an ethical and political problem and I would proceed on that theory." A little while later, after Baruch's attempt to recruit physicist Robert Oppenheimer to his delegation, Oppenheimer reported that Baruch spoke of "preparing the American people for a refusal by Russia."[8]

Baruch's team extensively rewrote the Acheson–Lilienthal Report. The new version—the Baruch Plan—allowed for private industry to engage in the mining and refining of fissionable materials.

To Acheson and his colleagues, two other changes to the original report were particularly damaging to the Baruch Plan's prospects of adoption at the United Nations. One change emphasized punishment for violators, including the possibility of nuclear attack.

Baruch had approached the United States Joint Chiefs of Staff with his ideas for punishing countries that violated the agreements only to find that while most senior American military officers generally supported the Acheson–Lilienthal Report, they opposed Baruch's changes to it. A letter from Admiral Nimitz was particularly clear:

I do not believe that the people of this country are prepared now to enter into an agreement for automatic punishment of other nations for acts which do not directly concern the United States. . . . If such punishment is dependent solely on the actual use of the bomb by a violator, the world catastrophe has already occurred; . . . we face the incongruity that the atomic bomb is necessary to enforce an agreement to outlaw its use.[9]

Baruch's response to the rebuff by the Joint Chiefs was to find a military advisor more to his liking in the person of General Leslie Groves

. Groves, in turn, selected additional advisors who supported American hegemony over nuclear weapons. One of those advisors was Edgar Sengier, the Belgian uranium miner, who warned that an international Atomic Development Authority would "upset wages [and] dissatisfy people" in the uranium mining business. Another of Grove's staff appointments was a major general whose twenty-year estimate of how long it would take the Soviets to build their own bomb just happened to coincide with Grove's own.[10] All in the Baruch camp believed that international control should be "entirely on American terms—or not at all."[11]

Baruch presented the plan before the UN General Assembly in June, 1946, where he intoned, "We are here to make a choice between the quick and the dead."[12]

In July of 1946, Truman's Secretary of Commerce, Henry Wallace, wrote a letter to the president that laid out the reasons why the Baruch Plan was so completely one-sided that it was unreasonable to expect the Russians to accept it. "How would it look to us," he asked, "if Russia had the atomic bomb and we did not, if Russia had 10,000-mile bombers and air bases within a thousand miles of our coastlines and we did not?" He pointed out the Baruch Plan required the Russians to cease their own atomic research "and to disclose their uranium and thorium resources while the United States retains the right to withhold its technical knowledge of atomic energy until the international control and inspection system is working to our satisfaction." Moreover, "we are telling the Russians that if they are 'good boys' we may eventually turn over our knowledge of atomic energy to them and to the other nations. . . . Is it any wonder that the Russians did not show any great enthusiasm for our plan?"[13]

Wallace went on to add that the Soviet Union had only "two cards which she can use in negotiating with us: (1) our lack of information on the state of her scientific and technical progress on atomic energy and (2) our ignorance of her uranium and thorium resources." Meanwhile, the United States has a "stockpile of bombs, manufacturing plants in actual production of B-29s and B-36s, and our bases covering half the globe. Yet we are in effect asking her to reveal her only two cards immediately—telling her that after we have seen her cards we will decide whether we want to continue to play the game."[14]

Despite the one-sided nature of the Baruch Plan, the Russians remained committed to negotiations through the summer and late into the fall, offering compromises on some points, even as the United States continued to build more bombs and conducted a bomb test in the South Pacific. When a Russian delegate to the UN suggested a meeting between Secretary of State Byrnes and Soviet Foreign Minister Molotov, a member of Baruch's delegation, Ferdinand Eberstadt, dismissed the idea with the rather odd comment that "further discussion would merely serve to take the focus off the Commission's work as such."[15]

Baruch and his associates demanded that the UN Security Council take a final vote on the plan by the end of the year. Ten of the twelve members of the Security Council voted in favor of the Baruch Plan. But rather than vote against it, the Soviet Union and Poland chose to abstain. Of course, without Soviet consent, the

Baruch Plan was essentially dead and Baruch resigned from the American delegation at the beginning of 1947.

Herken suggests that the Russians were more interested in delay than in any sincere effort to negotiate with the Baruch delegation. He also points out that Baruch's terms likely left America's Allies to suspect that they would be excluded from what Eberstadt called "*our* world."[16]

They could only wait to find out how America would use what Baruch called its "winning weapon."[17]

CHAPTER 7

The Pentagon Plans
to Use the Bomb

Despite the near hysteria over the "atomic secret" on the part of political leaders, the press, and the public at the end of World War II, America's military leaders had no clear strategy for the use of the atomic bomb in the postwar world. They responded by creating ever more elaborate plans for ever greater levels of casual destructiveness, a process that has continued to this day.

From 1946 to 1949, the Pentagon developed a series of atomic war plans, each with its own code name, including Pincher, Broiler, Grabber, Fleetwood, Dropshot, and Offtackle.

For much of this period, these plans were curiously disconnected from America's actual military capabilities. Even as late as spring 1947, the United States had no more than about a dozen atomic bombs, and none of them were ready for combat use. A study from that year stated, "It appears that the atomic bomb and future military requirements of fissionable materials cannot be met for a number of years." The situation only improved substantially toward the end of 1948. Most surprising of all was the finding of the 1947 study "that the Joint Chiefs of Staff had not been informed of the foregoing facts" about the supply of atomic bombs.[1]

The basic assumption behind all of these plans was that the Soviet Union intended to invade Western Europe and other areas along the Soviet border. If it did so, the massive Soviet army would overwhelm Western defenses. However, it didn't seem practical to simply drop atomic bombs on an enormous army dispersed over hundreds of miles of Western Europe, especially when the entire reason for the war was to defend the people of the very countries the Soviets might invade.

Thus, the plans all called for temporarily ceding territory to the Red Army and then relying on what had become the preferred option in World War II: attempting to destroy the enemy's morale by bombing its cities, which, in turn, would supposedly force him to withdraw from the territory he had taken. Only instead of using conventional weapons as it had done in World War II, the United States would use the atomic bombs against the cities of the Soviet Union in an attempt to force it to withdraw from the territory it had taken in Europe. In other words, from very early on in the atomic era, the United States was committed to a nuclear first strike against civilians.

A disturbing discrepancy remained between the goals of the civilian authorities who presumably controlled the nuclear weapons and the nature of the war plans developed by the military. One of the war plans, dubbed Fleetwood, called for a massive atomic bombing of Russian cities, including Moscow and Leningrad, that "could well lead to Soviet capitulation."[2] But, as Herken points out, such a massive attack could wipe out the entire Soviet leadership, leaving no one to implement a "capitulation":

> Remarkably, there seemed little appreciation in the ... plan of the possibilities for deterring further Soviet military operations ... and even less of a belief that the war could be limited. Nor did the plan appear to see the illogic of foreclosing tacit negotiations with the enemy by bombing his major cities and governmental centers at the outset. .... Not only diplomacy but even strategy itself ended if (or when) deterrence failed.[3]

Although in principle the decision to use atomic weapons could only be made by the president, the logic of nuclear war undermined his authority. As one State Department analyst pointed out: "If a war of major proportions breaks out, the National Military Establishment will have little alternative but to recommend to the Chief Executive that atomic weapons be used, and he will have no alternative [but] to go along."[4]

There were those who questioned whether it was even possible to execute such a plan. They also suggested that even if they were able to bomb Moscow and Leningrad, their success may not have a substantial effect on Russia's ability to wage war. Chief among them was Secretary of Defense James Forrestal, who wrote to Truman, "I do not believe that air power alone can win a war any more than an Army or naval power can win a war, and I do not believe in the theory that an atomic offensive will extinguish in a week the will to fight."[5]

Chief of Naval Operations Louis Denfeld also questioned the "ability of the Air Force successfully to deliver the bomb by means of unescorted missions flown by present-day bombers, deep into enemy territory in the face of strong Soviet air defenses, and to drop it on targets whose locations are not accurately known."[6]

James Forrestal shared similar concerns. In the fall of 1948, he commissioned two separate studies to examine the feasibility of the Pentagon's plan for an atomic attack against the Soviet Union. One was chaired by Army General John E. Hull, the other by Air Force General Hubert Harmon. The president ordered that the results of the Hull and Harmon studies be sent to him as soon as they were available.

The Harmon Report was completed in May 1949 and challenged many of the assumptions behind an air atomic attack against the Soviets. Even if, as the Pentagon assumed, all of the atomic bombs were dropped over their targets, the Soviets would still be able to weather the attack and regroup militarily. The report also suggested that rather than destroying the morale of the Russian people, "atomic bombing would validate Soviet propaganda . . . stimulate resentment against the United States, unify these people and increase their will to fight."[7]

Nor, the report found, would the attack stop a Red Army invasion of Western Europe or the Middle East. Defeating the Soviets would require a counterattack by Allied forces on the ground. Instead, the use of the atomic bomb "will produce certain psychological and retaliatory reactions detrimental to the achievement of Allied war objectives and its destructive effects will complicate post-hostilities problems." Worse yet, the first use of atomic weapons by the United States would set a precedent for the use of "any weapons of mass destruction."[8]

Strangely enough, the conclusions of the report ignored these findings. Instead, it supported the decision to use the bomb, stating that "the advantages of its early use would be transcending."[9]

The criticisms leveled by the Harmon report were not welcomed by the Joint Chiefs. By May, Truman had fired Secretary of Defense Forrestal and replaced him with Louis Johnson. But despite the president's orders that he receive a copy of the report, Johnson withheld it from the president.

Herken notes that the Hull report was even more critical of the Pentagon's plans than the Harmon report:

The Hull report cast serious doubt upon the ability of U.S. bombers to penetrate Soviet air defenses in sufficient numbers to deliver a stunning initial blow without incurring losses that would make a sustained air offensive impossible. Additional problems and oversights contained in existing air force warplanes—a shortage of aviation fuel and aircraft parts, for example, and the unanticipated vulnerability of bases in Britain—made the success of current war plans still more problematic.[10]

The Hull report was not sent to the president until January 1950. But by that time, no one in Washington was interested in evaluating how the United States might exploit its atomic monopoly. In mid-September 1949, rainwater samples taken in the United States showed that the Soviet Union had tested its own atomic bomb.

CHAPTER 8

The Soviet Union Builds a Bomb

oviet scientists were well aware of the experiments in Western Europe that showed that an atomic bomb was theoretically possible. However, Stalin began only a small research project in January 1943. Soviet scientists thought it unlikely that they would be able to build a bomb in time to affect the outcome of the war. They also knew that Britain and the United States were starting up extensive research programs of their own.[1] And although they were also aware that Germany was also attempting to build an atomic bomb, by the spring of that year, they had received reliable intelligence information that the German effort was not successful.

In his extensive study of the Soviet Union's development of its own atomic weapon, *Stalin and the Bomb*, David Holloway suggests the failure of Germany's bomb project reassured Stalin that he need not worry whether the atomic bomb would be a factor in his war with Germany. At the urging of Soviet physicists, Stalin did, however, start a relatively modest effort to build a bomb. Holloway explains that the "project he started is best understood as a rather small hedge against future uncertainties."[2]

The Soviet effort was hampered by the lack of access to enough uranium for basic research, let alone actual bomb development. But the Soviet program was helped along when, starting in late 1943, a German informant named Klaus Fuchs began working at the

Manhattan Project. He sent the Soviets reports on critical research results and detailed design specifications for the construction of the American plutonium bomb, the same design as the one eventually used against Nagasaki.[3]

By the time Germany surrendered in May of 1945, Soviet scientists already had in hand intelligence information from Fuchs showing that the United States' atomic bomb was likely to become a reality in the near future. They wrote to the Soviet leaders urging their research be given "the most favorable and advantageous conditions."[4] There was no response to the scientists' memorandum, perhaps because of the Soviet leaders' deep distrust of both their intelligence agents and their scientists.

Lavrentiy Beria, the head of the Soviet secret police, the NKVD, distrusted the intelligence reports from Fuchs. The fact that Germany's effort to build a bomb had failed may have reinforced his suspicions that the United States, Fuchs, or both were deceiving him.

Beria suspected the United States was trying to lure the Soviet Union into an enormous expenditure on a project that could never succeed. Moreover, other scientists who had not written in favor of building a bomb had said that such an undertaking would take a very long time. Beria told one of his agents who ran the Soviet spy operation in the United States, "If this is disinformation, I'll put you all in the cellar."[5]

As Holloway explains,

In spite of Fuchs's report that the United States was planning to test the bomb on July 10, and to use it against Japan . . . [Soviet leaders did not understand] the role that the atomic bomb would soon play in international relations. If they had seen the connection between the bomb and foreign policy, they would surely have provided [the atomic bomb project] with more active support. Their failure to do so suggests that the atomic bomb had no reality for them in the summer of 1945, that they had no conception of the impact it was about to have on world politics.[6]

The destruction of Hiroshima demonstrated to Stalin the power of the atomic bomb as both a weapon of war and a powerful force in international diplomacy, but his most immediate focus was the Far East. He had already been concerned during the summer of 1945 that the United States and Britain hoped to defeat Japan before Russia could enter the war there, thus preventing Stalin from reclaiming territory near Japan as agreed to at Yalta. These were areas Russia had once held but lost to Japan in the Russo–Japanese War of 1905. Retaking these areas was important to Stalin both for geopolitical reasons and as a matter of national pride.

The atomic bombings of Hiroshima and Nagasaki heightened his concerns. He ordered his army to invade Manchuria as soon as possible and proceed toward Japan, and the Red Army quickly captured much of the territory it had lost in the Russo–Japanese War. Stalin was preparing to take over part of Hokkaido, the northernmost island of Japan, in the hopes of reducing American influence in shaping the future of the country. But he backed off, wishing to avoid a possible political conflict with the United States, perhaps even an armed confrontation.

As it was, Stalin had attained his primary goal, announcing that "the [Japanese] surrender means that southern Sakhalin and the Kurile islands [sic] will pass to the Soviet Union, and from now on will not serve as a means for isolating the Soviet Union from the ocean or as a base for Japanese attacks on our Far East."[7]

Nonetheless, Stalin realized the Soviet Union had to build its own bomb. Although most American historians have seen America's atomic strike against Japan as an attempt to end the war as quickly as possible, Stalin could not help but suspect that Truman's motivation had a lot to do with thwarting the Soviet

Union's ambitions in the Far East. As noted earlier, there is evidence that his suspicion may have been well founded.

Stalin also realized the implications of the atomic bomb extended well beyond the end of the war. He was reported to have told two of his chief nuclear scientists a few days after the atomic bombing of Hiroshima, "Hiroshima has shaken the whole world. The balance has been destroyed."[8] According to Andrei Gromyko, the Soviet ambassador to Washington, Stalin conjectured that once the United States had built the bomb, America would try to use its atomic monopoly to impose its will over Europe, the Soviet Union, and the rest of the world. But, Stalin added, "No, that will not be."[9] At that point, Stalin viewed the bomb as a potent symbol of power as well as a military threat. He ordered that the Soviet atomic bomb project be given top priority.

One indication of the importance Stalin attached to the atomic bomb project after Hiroshima is the person he put in charge of it: Lavrentiy Beria. Beria knew nothing about physics, but he was an excellent manager. And as head of the secret police, the NKVD, he was second only to Stalin as the most feared person in the Soviet Union. As one of Beria's former colleagues in the Soviet leadership put it: "Just one remark like 'Beria has ordered . . .' worked absolutely without fail."[10]

Despite the information they had obtained from Klaus Fuchs concerning the design of the American atomic bomb, the Soviets had to surmount a number of logistic and technical problems before they could build their own. These problems could correspond with the second and third parts of the "atomic secret" Truman described in his speech in October 1945: In addition to the common theoretical knowledge of the physics of atomic energy, the engineering knowledge to build an atomic bomb was also necessary, along with the "combination of industrial capacity and resources necessary to produce the bomb" cited by Truman.

Initially, the biggest problem for the Soviet scientists was the lack of uranium, without which they could carry out almost none of the research or build none of the necessary infrastructure, let alone build an actual bomb. The uranium deposits in Germany and Czechoslovakia solved the supply problem, at least initially. But they still had to set up mining operations and facilities to process the ore before it could be sent to the Soviet Union.

They then had to refine the ore to produce metallic uranium that in turn could be used to produce the plutonium core of an atomic bomb. Publicly available information from the United States provided some basic information about these processes, but the Soviet scientists had to undertake considerable experimentation and development of their own before they could build full-scale production plants for uranium metal and nuclear reactors to produce the plutonium. They needed to create the "atomic industry."[11]

Eventually, the Soviets built a large production facility near the city of Cheliabinsk in the Ural Mountains. Construction began in autumn of 1946 and was completed in late 1947. Much of the work was done by prisoners, with as many of 70,000 of them working at the same time.[12]

The development of the Soviet atomic bomb was a remarkable achievement for a war-ravaged country that had only a fraction of the industrial and technical infrastructure of the United States even before the start of the war. Stalin was able to compensate for those deficits in part by using forced labor, not only at Cheliabinsk but also at the uranium mines in Czechoslovakia and Germany.[13]

Perhaps most importantly, the Soviet Union had a talented and sophisticated cadre of physicists who had kept up with developments in atomic physics before the war. After the war, the Soviets also employed a number of German scientists who chose to work in the Soviet Union, but for the most part, they did not make a major contribution to the atomic project.[14]

The design specifications for the American bomb supplied by Klaus Fuchs did make a substantial contribution to Soviet efforts.

The best-informed estimates are that Fuch's intelligence reports saved the Soviet Union one to two years of research and development. Still, in 1951, the Soviets tested a uranium-235 bomb that required a completely different design from the one Fuchs provided.[15]

The Soviet scientists also made use of a public report about the making of America's atomic bomb, which was published just six days after the bombing of Hiroshima as part of a public relations program. The report, titled *Atomic Energy for Military Purposes*, became known as the Smyth Report[16] after its author, Henry DeWolf Smyth, a Princeton physics professor who worked on the early stages of the bomb's development.

According to an account from the United States Department of Energy, the report was published "to both allay inordinate inquisitiveness and satisfy the legitimate public need to know." They also believed "from the standpoint of security, the release of some selected information would make it easier to maintain the secrecy of the highly classified aspects of the project."[17]

However, the Soviets acquired a copy, promptly translated it into Russian, and in early 1946 printed 30,000 copies. The Smyth Report provided them with "an overall picture of what the United States had done" and "exercised an important influence on the technical choices made in the Soviet project."[18]

Soviet researchers made technical decisions in several specific areas based on information from the Smyth Report: the design of the experimental reactor, the power output requirements for a nuclear reactor to create plutonium, and the methods of separating newly created plutonium from uranium in a nuclear reactor.[19] The Smyth Report also described how at one point, frustrated by the meager output from the method they were using to purify uranium, the Americans used a purification method that the Soviets knew about but had little experience with. The Russians then said to themselves, "'What the Americans can do, we can do too,' and adapted the . . . method for use on an industrial scale."[20]

Ironically, General Leslie Groves enthusiastically endorsed the writing and publication of the Smyth Report. Groves also wrote the foreword:

> All pertinent scientific information which can be released to the public at this time without violating the needs of national security is contained in this volume. No requests for additional information should be made to private persons or organizations associated directly or indirectly with the project. Persons disclosing or securing additional information by any means whatsoever without authorization are subject to severe penalties under the Espionage Act.[21]

Although the information from America, whether in the form of espionage or public releases, helped the Soviet scientists make rapid progress, the suspicions of their political overseers were a constant threat to their project and even to their own personal well-being.

For the NKVD officials, seeing was believing, and whatever they could not see was immediately suspect. This made for a difficult relationship with the physicists who were working with invisible forces whose effects would eventually only become visible in the form of a massive explosion. Worse yet, the visible evidence would appear only after a long development period during which progress could only be inferred rather than witnessed directly.

In 1949 a group of Beria's senior secret police officials arrived at Cheliabinsk while a senior scientist was preparing a hemisphere of plutonium to be used in the bomb. The scientist recalled,

> They asked what I was doing.... "Why do you think it is plutonium?" I said that I knew the whole technical process for obtaining it and was therefore sure that it was plutonium ... "But why are you sure some piece of iron hasn't been substituted for it?" I held up a piece to the alpha-counter, and it began to

crackle at once. . . . "But perhaps it has just been rubbed with plutonium on the outside and that is why it crackles," said someone. . . . I grew angry, took that piece and held it out to them: "Feel it, it's hot!" One of them said that it did not take long to heat a piece of iron. Then I responded that he could sit and look till morning and check whether the plutonium remained hot. But I would go to bed. This apparently convinced them, and they went away.[22]

The danger to the scientists posed by this kind of suspicion was greatly increased by the postwar resurgence of an ideological assault against Western science that had been a significant factor in Soviet politics in the 1930s. That previous movement had been confined largely to the biological sciences. But with the growing postwar rift with their former allies, Soviet leaders were open to the notion that Western physics was also contaminated by false ways of thinking and was thus an outgrowth of degenerate Western culture.

In May of 1947 Stalin commented that "the scientific intelligentsia, professors, physicians . . . have an insufficiently educated feeling of Soviet patriotism." This presumed lack of patriotism became associated with the highly abstract and often counterintuitive concepts of quantum mechanics and relativity. The head of the Ministry of Higher Education wrote, "Physics is taught . . . without regard to dialectical materialism. . . . Instead of decisively unmasking trends which are inimical to Marxism–Leninism, some of our scientists frequently adopt idealist positions, which are making their way into higher educational establishments through physics."[23]

A group of less-accomplished physicists who were not working on the bomb attempted to use the changing political atmosphere to undermine the position of their colleagues who were working on the atomic bomb. They accused the atomic bomb scientists of "grovelling before the West," claiming, "It is necessary to root out mercilessly every hint of open cosmopolitanism, which is

Anglo-American imperialism's ideological weapon of diversion," and to avoid "uncritically receiving Western physical theories and propagandizing them in our country."[24]

Beria asked the director of the Soviet atomic bomb project if it was true that quantum mechanics and relativity conflicted with the materialist tenets of Marxism-Leninism. The director replied that without quantum mechanics and relativity theory, there would be no bomb. Beria eventually approached Stalin to ask what should be done about the less accomplished physicists who were challenging the legitimacy of the bomb project. "Leave them in peace. We can always shoot them later."[25]

CHAPTER 9

The Berlin Airlift

While the nuclear arms race broke into public view with the Soviet atomic bomb test of 1949, the first open instance of atomic diplomacy took place over a year earlier with the Berlin Blockade.

In April 1948 the Soviets began harassing Western traffic crossing through East Germany toward Berlin. The military governor of the U.S. Zone in Germany, General Lucius Clay, told Truman that he intended to order American guards to fire at Soviet soldiers if they attempted to enter American trains. Although deeply alarmed by the Soviet harassment, Truman quickly countermanded General Clay. But he did order the Joint Chiefs to review war plans because of the "suddenly urgent immediate issues" raised by the Soviet actions.[1]

After a period of increasing restrictions on Western access to the city, the Russians began a total blockade on June 23. Lacking any practical way of challenging the Russian actions, Clay advocated sending an armored military column across the Soviet Zone to Berlin, while LeMay, who was then commander of the U.S. Air Forces in Europe, wanted to bomb Soviet troops manning the blockade.[2]

The Secretary of the Army Kenneth Royall wanted the United States to "have several A-bombs available (in England and elsewhere) for immediate use . . . such use [to] be left entirely to the military." He advocated such a full-scale nuclear escalation despite

Truman's warning:

> You have got to understand that this isn't a military weapon.
> It is used to wipe out women and children and unarmed
> people, and not for military uses. . . . You have got to under-
> stand that I have got to think about the effect of such a thing
> on international relations. This is no time to be juggling an
> atom bomb around.[3]

But Truman did end up "juggling" atomic bombs; he just didn't
do it openly. His response to the Soviet blockade was to trans-
fer B-29 bombers that the Soviets knew were capable of carrying
atomic weapons to bases in England from which the planes could
reach Russia in a move that Secretary of State George Marshall
characterized as "the atomic-age equivalent of gunboat diplomacy."[4]

With the total blockade in place, the United States expanded an
earlier effort that had used the B-29s to provide basic supplies to
civilians in West Berlin. This expansion of the B-29 flights became
known as the Berlin Airlift. The Berlin Airlift is still celebrated in
the United States as an American triumph over the Soviet commu-
nists' perfidious behavior. Although the implied atomic threat is
not nearly as well known, it stands as an important marker for the
beginning of the Cold War. With the success of the Berlin Airlift,
John Foster Dulles suggested, "We have won round one with the
Russians."[5]

Yet the atomic threat was largely a ruse. No bombs were actually
sent to England, nor were any technicians capable of preparing
them for use. The B-29s, although technically "atomic capable,"
required modifications before they could actually deliver a bomb,
and those modifications had not been carried out.[6]

Although Stalin recognized the implied nuclear threat in the
presence of the B-29s, he did not believe the United States would
use atomic bombs in the conflict over West Berlin. In his memoirs,

Stalin's deputy foreign minister at the time, Andrei Gromyko, commented, "I believe that Stalin—of course nobody actually asked him directly—embarked on that affair in the certain knowledge that the . . . American administration was not run by frivolous people who would start a nuclear war over such a situation."[7]

Stalin had his own geopolitical considerations that led to his starting the blockade. In March 1948, the United States, Britain, and France announced that they were combining their separate jurisdictions in Germany to form a single political entity. The Soviets protested that this move violated the Potsdam Agreement, which called for a unified German state. The Soviets began the total blockade on June 24, a few days after the Western Allies announced the creation of a separate German currency, the Deutsche Mark. The Russians responded by creating their own new currency to be used in their sector of Berlin.[8]

The Soviet leadership's thinking seemed to be a mirror image of their American counterparts; Stalin wanted to "force the Western powers either to give up their moves towards a separate West German state, or to relinquish West Berlin" because "if the Western powers were able to set up a West German state unopposed, they would see the Soviet Union as a weak opponent and be encouraged to pursue a more active policy. It was important for the Soviet Union to take a stand."[9] In his memoirs, Nikita Khrushchev wrote that they were "prodding the capitalist world with the tip of a bayonet."[10]

In the end, Stalin decided that allowing the conflict with the Western Allies to escalate was not worth the risk. However, there were limits to his forbearance. Gromyko believed Stalin would have resisted a military assault against Russian forces of the sort Clay and LeMay advocated for.[11]

The Berlin Blockade of 1948 set the framework in which the United States and the Soviet Union engaged in a complex game of nuclear intimidation, or what Dulles called "neither war, nor peace."[12]

CHAPTER 10

A Cold Warrior

In August 1945, a fourteen-year-old boy named Daniel Ellsberg was standing on a corner in downtown Detroit when he looked at the front page of the *Detroit News*. The headline announced that the United States had used a single bomb to destroy an entire Japanese city. Unlike the vast majority of Americans at the time, Ellsberg already knew what an atomic bomb was and what its implications were for the future.

The previous fall a teacher had told his class about articles that had appeared in the popular press, such as the *Saturday Evening Post*, describing research that had been done before the war. The research showed that by splitting uranium atoms, it might be possible to create an enormously powerful explosion. The teacher then suggested the class explore what the implications might be if such bombs were actually created. The students all agreed that such a development would be a disaster for humanity; it didn't matter what country got there first. "Mankind could not handle such a destructive force. It could not be safely controlled. The power would be 'abused'—that is, used dangerously, with terrible consequences."[1]

Today Daniel Ellsberg is best known for his 1971 release of the Pentagon Papers, a classified history of the Vietnam War that had been commissioned by the Department of Defense. Ellsberg had access to the study by virtue of the top-secret classification he held through his position as a senior consultant at the RAND Corporation, a major military contractor. The release of the Pentagon Papers set off a chain of events that eventually led to President Nixon's resignation and helped hasten the end of America's war in Vietnam.

Ellsberg worked at RAND from the late 1950s until 1970. During that period, he also worked in the Pentagon as special assistant to the Assistant Secretary of Defense for International Security Affairs and spent two years working in South Vietnam as a member of the State Department. His primary area of expertise was nuclear war strategy, an odd choice for someone who would later risk a lengthy prison term by turning the Pentagon Papers over to the public. But in the late 1940s and early 1950s, like his "older colleagues at that time and like so many among my generation in America," Ellsberg had become a self-described "Cold Warrior."[2] Looking back, he says he never lost his "well-founded abhorrence of the domestic tyranny of Stalinist-style regimes—whether in the Soviet Union and Eastern Europe, China, North Korea, Vietnam, or Cuba." But "more problematic . . . in fact, I would now say, flat wrong, recklessly so—was the presumption that such regimes, like Nazism, had an insatiable appetite for expansion" and "posed a direct military threat to Western Europe and America."[3]

His 2017 memoir, *The Doomsday Machine: Confessions of a Nuclear War Planner*, gives us an insider's account of the serpentine logic of America's civilian and military nuclear war planning establishment during the 1950s and 60s. Unfortunately, this isn't just a historical episode that came to an end along with the Cold War. The Doomsday Machine Ellsberg describes is still in place today.

One of Ellsberg's first assignments with RAND was to analyze how a decision to launch a nuclear attack would actually be carried out under the plans then in place. This was in 1960, when there were very few intercontinental ballistic missiles and the nuclear attack force consisted mostly of aircraft. The Pentagon wanted Ellsberg to examine how an Execute command to begin a nuclear attack would reach bomber groups on the Pacific Rim before they could be destroyed by a Soviet attack.

But the problem Ellsberg took a personal interest in "was the obverse of that one: reducing the possibility of *unauthorized* action. How to assure that no subordinate would be inclined or able to launch the forces under his control in the absence of an authorization from his superiors or the president?"[4]

Contrary to what most Americans have been led to believe, the president is not the only person who can authorize a nuclear attack. That fact becomes immediately obvious once one realizes that a single nuclear bomb can wipe out all of Washington D.C., including the president, his or her cabinet, the Joint Chiefs of Staff, and much of Congress. A few more bombs could destroy the communications infrastructure used to relay a strike message to military forces within or beyond America's borders.

If an enemy believed that such a sudden "decapitation" attack could eliminate America's ability to respond, that enemy might be tempted to take advantage of that fact. The Commander in Chief of American forces in the Pacific, Admiral Harry Felt, told Ellsberg that for this reason, Eisenhower had sent secret letters to senior commanders such as Felt authorizing them to initiate an Execute command on their own, if they believed they had lost communications with Washington because of a sudden nuclear attack.[5]

It made sense that Eisenhower would have sent it to them given the circumstances. Did those senior officers delegate the authority to commanders below them? And if so, just how far down the chain of command did this subdelegation go?

What Ellsberg found was that the senior officers did indeed authorize their subordinates to launch an attack, and these subordinates, in turn, delegated that authority to officers below them. "It was clear," wrote Ellsberg, "that the same incentives that influenced the president existed for further delegation by lower commanders" because "each level of command had reason to worry that during a crisis, an outage of communications, whether due to atmospheric or technical difficulties or an enemy attack on [its] command headquarters, could paralyze the nuclear capabilities of subordinate units unless they'd been delegated authority to act under such conditions."[6]

Ellsberg had been talking only to military officials in the Pacific Command, but it was clear to him that the same logic would apply to the American military all over the world. He felt that allowing lower-level military officers to use nuclear weapons on their own put the decision in the hands of officers with "lesser experience and maturity; and narrower responsibilities and access to information." Moreover, as one went down the chain of command, the decision covered "smaller portions of the overall retaliatory forces." Ellsberg wrote:

> To a commander at the lower level, whose mission understandably seemed to him to have transcendent importance if it involved any nuclear weapons at all, it wouldn't look that way. He would want to be sure that "his" weapons took part in the big war—the fight for national survival and victory.[7]

In a sense, this cascading delegation of authority to use nuclear weapons was something that might be expected in a bureaucratic setting, where the people in charge of each segment of the organization seek to maximize their ability to carry out what they see as its mission, however narrow their view of that mission might be. Of course, this situation was much more serious than the sort of bureaucratic dysfunction that seems to be an inescapable part of modern life.

Concerned that so many people had the ability to initiate a nuclear attack, whether authorized or not, Ellsberg traveled to some bases in the eastern Pacific to observe nuclear security practices firsthand. What he found was even more disturbing than he had first imagined it might be.

His first stop was at an air force base in Okinawa, where he investigated how local commanders conducted training and preparedness exercises. He found that the crews drilled by jumping into their planes and starting them up. But they never even taxied to the runway to prepare for takeoff, nor did they take off and head to their rendezvous point, where they were to circle and wait for the final authorization to deliver their weapons to their assigned targets. If they did not receive that authorization after a specified amount of time, they were supposed to return to their base. This provision was known as the "fail-safe procedure."[8]

However, the pilots were never told whether the orders to start their planes was or was not part of a drill. Ellsberg was also disturbed by the fact that the drills never went to the next step in which the pilots would proceed to the rendezvous point:

> That said to me that if they were ordered to take off from those pads, it would be an extraordinary, perhaps unprecedented, experience for the alert pilots. Even if it was in fact—unknown to them—only a drill, the first time or two that it happened would almost surely lead them to infer that "this was it." An enemy attack was under way or else they were leading a preemptive strike. At the least, they would have to infer that the indications of enemy attack were more serious than they ever had been before. It would be in that state of mind that they would head for their rendezvous areas, even if they received no Execute order to follow their launch order.[9]

The situation could become much more perilous if the flights came during an international crisis, such as those that occurred over the offshore islands of Quemoy and Matsu, which were (and still are) the subjects of competing territorial claims by mainland

China and Taiwan. Two such crises had already occurred. The first took place in 1954 and 1955, the second in 1958. In both cases, the United States had prepared to use nuclear weapons.[10]

Base commanders were reluctant to send their pilots on drills to their rendezvous points. The reason for their reluctance made the situation even more alarming. As Ellsberg explains:

> Each of the alert planes, single-person F-100s, was carrying a Mark 28 thermonuclear weapon outside the plane, beneath the undercarriage. These weapons, we were told, were designed to be carried inside a plane for greater safety. But there was no room for that in these tactical fighter-bombers.[11]

Still worse, the bombs were not "one-point safe." Each of these bombs contained an atomic bomb like the one dropped on Nagasaki, which served as a trigger for the much larger thermonuclear hydrogen bomb. Not being one-point safe meant that if they were accidentally dropped or there was a fire or explosion, they could detonate either partially or totally. That's why, even though the risk was small, base commanders were reluctant to chance sending pilots out on drills.

> If a number of these planes actually taxied to the runway and took off in a great rush, one or more of them might bump into another or otherwise turn over, burn and explode, and produce a huge explosion, spreading lethal radioactivity over a large area, and just possibly, a nuclear fireball.[12]

But as Ellsberg points out, they would have to take the risk if there was a real alert. In that case, how would a pilot who had successfully taken off after never having done so in a drill react if he saw a mushroom cloud rising over the base behind him? He would already be primed to believe that this may not be a drill, and that what he had seen was the result of an enemy attack. He might then decide to complete his attack mission since there was no point in waiting for an Execute message from a base that no longer existed.[13]

Okinawa, where Ellsberg conducted his initial inquiry, was near the center of the American Pacific Command. He decided to investigate the situation at a more remote site. He chose the northernmost American base in the Pacific at Kunsan in South Korea. Kunsan was close enough to the Russian border that if any of its bombers took to the air, they would be immediately detected by Russian radar and their launch might be interpreted as an attack. For that reason, the Kunsan base commander was under a strict directive not to send his planes into the air unless he received explicit orders from central command in Seoul or Tokyo.

Nevertheless, the commander told Ellsberg that if there was a break in communications during an intense crisis such as the one over Quemoy, he "might well" order his planes in the air without orders from his superiors. Ellsberg notes this was an "era when an outage of communications from natural disturbances was a fairly frequent phenomenon . . . all over the Pacific" and, according to the Kunsan commander, occurred about once a day at his base. There had also been large-scale disruptions to military communications in the Pacific and on the U.S. mainland due to man-made accidents and natural causes.[14]

Ellsberg asked the Kunsan commander how he thought his pilots would react if they were at the rendezvous point but unable to communicate with their commanders and didn't receive an Execute message.

"Oh, I think they'd come back." Pause. "Most of them."

The last three words didn't register with me right away because before they were out of his mouth, my head was exploding . . . a voice inside was screaming, "Think? You *think* they'd come back?!" . . .

[The commander] added, "Of course, if one of them were to break out of that circle and go for his target, I think the rest would follow." He paused again; then he added reflectively, "And they might as well. If one goes, they might as well all go. I tell them not to do it though."[15]

After his experience at Kunsan, Ellsberg went on to wonder if "one subordinate individual, on his own initiative" could issue an Execute command to launch a nuclear attack. He soon found out that the answer was "yes."

The procedure by which nuclear bomber pilots were directed to attack their targets was code-named Spark Plug. Each pilot carried with him an envelope that contained another envelope inside of it. If he received an Execute command, he was to compare the first part of the code that accompanied the message with a sequence written on the outside of his envelope. If the two were identical he was to open the envelope and look at the sequence on the outside of the second envelope. If the second part of the code matched, he was to open the envelope, where he would find a card containing the last part. If that part matched, the pilot was to send a radio signal to the other planes in his group with the full launch code. The assumption was that, given the unreliable radio reception, he may have been the only one to receive the message. He was then supposed to fly to his target and drop his bomb.

Ellsberg also determined that the codes were the same for all planes and were changed infrequently if at all. Therefore, simply by opening his envelopes and reading the contents, a single rogue pilot could signal an entire set of bombers to attack their targets.[16]

When Ellsberg raised this possibility at various air bases in the Pacific Command, no one had thought of it, but they all agreed it was a realistic scenario. At first the typical response was that a rogue pilot couldn't convince his colleagues to join him in an unauthorized attack because he wouldn't know the entire authentication code.

> I would pause at this point, waiting to hear a second thought expressed (which never occurred). Then I would say offhandedly: "Unless he opened the envelopes."
> Even this hint often failed to turn a light on. I'd hear: "But that's against his orders. If he hasn't gotten the whole signal, he *can't* open it."
> That answer usually hung in the air only a moment or so.[17]

In principle, the issuance of an Execute command was more tightly controlled at command posts. Two officers, each with access to only part of the code, were to be on duty at all times. In practice, two officers were not always available. Ellsberg recounts how "officers would tell me . . . 'off the record' but with some pride . . . that they had conscientiously and sometimes ingeniously managed to assure that the system would work (to 'Go') even if they or their partner didn't happen to be on hand at the crucial moment."

One might assume the responses Ellsberg encountered were simply another particularly dangerous example of the bureaucratic blindness that is endemic to large organizations. But even if that were the case, the fact remains that the military commanders all the way up to highest levels were more interested in making sure they could launch a nuclear attack than they were in preventing an unauthorized one.[18]

When the Minuteman intercontinental ballistic missile was developed in the early 1960s, Secretary of Defense Robert McNamara ordered the military to install a locking feature on the Minuteman so that it couldn't be fired without a code sent from higher headquarters. Unbeknownst to McNamara, the Air Force circumvented his directive. As Bruce Blair, a former Minuteman launch control officer, reported:

> The Strategic Air Command (SAC) in Omaha quietly de-
> cided to set the "locks" to all zeros in order to circumvent
> this safeguard. . . . Our launch checklist in fact instructed
> us, the firing crew, to double-check the locking panel in our
> underground launch bunker to ensure that no digits other
> than zero had been inadvertently dialed into the panel. SAC
> remained far less concerned about unauthorized launches
> than about the potential of these safeguards to interfere with
> the implementation of wartime launch orders. And so the
> "secret unlock code" during the height of the nuclear crises
> of the Cold War remained constant at 00000000.[19]

After he left the air force in 1974, Blair campaigned to have the
locks properly configured. They were finally activated in 1977.

Ellsberg writes that throughout the Cold War, in addition to
placing more importance on being able to launch a nuclear attack than preventing unauthorized action, military commanders
believed the response to a warning of nuclear attack should be
immediate in order to destroy the enemy's weapons before they
could destroy America's ability to launch its own nuclear response.
Safety devices and procedures could lead to delay and were thus
incompatible with their mission as they saw it.[20]

One thing that became apparent to Ellsberg was that contrary
to what the citizens of the United States have been led to believe,
the people in control of the American military felt their behavior
should be unconstrained by the directives of civil authorities up to
and including the president. Several officers told Ellsberg:

> [The] reason . . . for the Joint Chiefs of Staff to tolerate
> the shortcomings of the control system, to put up fierce
> and prolonged resistance to measures that would tighten

control of nuclear weapons up and down the line . . . was their distrust, above all in a crisis, of the judgment of civilian commanders . . . to launch nuclear attacks when military commanders believed them to be urgently necessary.[21]

This is not to say the military leaders were united in their views when it came to nuclear war policy and practice. Frequent and often bitter conflicts were to be found within the military branches over what role each was to play if a war should break out . . . and therefore which branch should receive the most funding.

One such battle was fought over the circumstances under which the United States would launch an all-out nuclear strike against the Soviet Union. The Joint Chiefs used the term *general war*, which was in turn defined as "armed conflict," in their secret operational plan for initiating and carrying out such an attack. This definition was quite broad. "It implied that any conflict pitting U.S. forces against any more than several battalions of Soviet troops anywhere in the world—Iran, Korea, the Middle East, Indochina—would lead to instant U.S. strategic attacks on every city and command center in the Soviet Union *and* [italics in the original] China."[22]

President Eisenhower supported this all-or-nothing strategy on the assumption that anything beyond a minor skirmish between the United States and the Soviet Union would quickly escalate to a nuclear conflict. Therefore, the United States should strike first to maintain its nuclear advantage.

The army challenged this definition, arguing that the United States should plan for a wider range of military encounters without necessarily assuming they would immediately result in a nuclear war. To do otherwise was to ensure that a conflict that might have been resolved would inevitably result in the total destruction of both sides.

But Ellsberg notes:

To the layperson, this might appear sensible enough. But what Eisenhower, the Air Force, and successive chairmen of the JCS detected behind these innocent-sounding definitions was a charter for the Army to go to their allies in Congress to seek capabilities for fighting even multiple Soviet divisions in a limited, non-nuclear, and non-general war. That was precisely what the budget-obsessed President Eisenhower and the Army's service rivals feared and wanted to avoid.[23]

The concerns about fighting "multiple Soviet divisions" were probably unfounded. The intelligence estimates from both the United States and NATO greatly exaggerated the size and strength of Soviet forces in Europe. For example, of the 175 Soviet divisions often cited in those intelligence reports, many of them had few soldiers or equipment assigned to them and in some cases none at all.[24]

Nonetheless, there was a substantial Soviet presence in East Germany, and the funds needed to confront this presence would have come out of the air force and navy budgets. This budgetary cost to the air force and navy might have been worth it if it reduced the likelihood of total nuclear war.

As it was, American nuclear war planning seemed locked into a pattern that was established in the immediate postwar years when the United States was the sole nuclear power. The Pentagon's plans from that time—Pincher, Broiler, Grabber, and their immediate descendants—all relied on that nuclear monopoly; like their counterparts a decade later, these plans also assumed that nuclear weapons would be a cheaper alternative to building and maintaining a large conventional military force in Europe and elsewhere. However morally dubious such a strategy may have been, its immediate "cost" to the United States—and indeed the entire world—beyond its budgetary aspect was much lower at the beginning of the Cold War in the late 1940s than it was a decade later.

CHAPTER 11

Missiles in Cuba

While John Foster Dulles's characterization of the Cold War as "neither war, nor peace" seems apt, it is hardly reassuring. Like a ball that has reached its apogee, it may appear to be still for a brief moment, but it must eventually come down somewhere. With the Cuban Missile Crisis of October 1962, it very nearly descended into war.

On Monday, October 22, President Kennedy went on television to announce that the Soviet Union was installing nuclear-capable "offensive" ballistic missiles in Cuba. He also announced a naval blockade against Cuba that he called a "quarantine," a euphemism to cover over the fact that a blockade was an act of war. He also issued a threat of all-out nuclear war when he stated that if a single missile from Cuba was launched "against any nation in the Western Hemisphere," the United States would respond with "a full retaliatory response upon the Soviet Union."[1]

The Soviets were installing medium- and intermediate-range ballistic missiles in Cuba, more than enough for a "decapitation" strike against Washington and the United States' strategic command center in Omaha. And although the Soviet Union's nuclear strike capabilities were far behind those of the United States, they already had the ability to accomplish the same thing without relying on missiles in Cuba, and they were rapidly increasing the power and reach of their nuclear arsenal independent of their actions in Cuba.

American war planners had never assumed that Washington or other command centers in the country would survive an initial Soviet attack. That was why the United States had created the elaborate system of delegated authority Ellsberg had examined a few years earlier. A nuclear attack from Cuba could not prevent a completely devastating response, and the Soviets were well aware of that fact.

Secretary of Defense McNamara had come to the same conclusion. At a meeting of the Executive Committee of the National Security Council (ExComm), he told the president, "I'll be quite frank, I don't think there *is* [italics in the original] a military problem. . . . This is a domestic political problem."[2]

Whatever his geopolitical goals may have been, Khrushchev had seriously overreached in terms of his military position. His forces were thousands of miles away from home, and his missiles in Cuba were just ninety miles away from the United States' massive military forces. Neither he nor the Cubans could long resist a conventional military attack by the Americans, and it seemed unlikely that he would be willing to risk a nuclear war to defend his new adventure in Cuba.

Khrushchev appeared to have come to the same realization. On Friday evening, October 26, he sent the United States a telegram which Robert Kennedy described as "very long and emotional." He proposed a settlement whereby

> we for our part, will declare that our ships bound for Cuba are not carrying any armaments. You will declare that the United States will not invade Cuba with its troops and will not support any other forces that might intend to invade Cuba. Then the necessity of the presence of our military specialists in Cuba will disappear.[3]

But there was a confusing complication. The next morning

another message arrived from Khrushchev demanding that the United States also withdraw the intermediate ballistic missiles it had placed in Turkey. Kennedy decided to send an oral message to Khrushchev via Soviet ambassador Dobrynin that if the Soviets removed the missiles from Cuba, the United States would subsequently remove its missiles from Turkey, provided the Soviets make no public statement about the American withdrawal of its missiles in Turkey.[4]

A dangerous new complication arose on Saturday when a Soviet surface-to-air missile (SAM) shot down an American U-2 surveillance plane over Cuba. Contrary to his previous assurances to the Joint Chiefs of Staff that if any reconnaissance plane were to be shot down, the minimum American response would be to attack Cuban air defense sites, Kennedy decided to adhere to his decision to wait for Khrushchev's response.[5]

On Sunday morning, Radio Moscow announced that the Soviet Union had begun removing the missiles from Cuba. There was no mention of the U.S. missiles in Turkey.

To Daniel Ellsberg, who had come to Washington from California to provide staff assistance to the ExComm at the beginning of the crisis, the "chance of *nuclear* [italics in the original] war erupting from this confrontation was extremely low." He heard that the members of the ExComm had put chances of a nuclear war at one in a hundred. One of Ellsberg's colleagues had suggested odds of one in a thousand. But the day after the crisis ended, Paul Nitze, an Assistant Secretary of Defense, told Ellsberg that he had put the odds at one in ten.[6]

Years later, Robert McNamara commented that on October 27, "the Saturday before the Sunday in which Khrushchev announced the withdrawal of the missiles . . . and a U-2 was shot down . . . I remember leaving the White House at the end of that Saturday. It was a beautiful fall day. And thinking that might well be the last sunset I saw. You couldn't tell what was going to follow." He feared that "those of us who had fought hard to avoid a military strike against Cuba had prevailed up to that point" but that they might not be able to continue to do so if the Soviets refused to remove the missiles. "And those who had recommended military action in the first instance had always been forthright enough to say that they didn't know how it would end."[7]

McNamara's big fear wasn't that the Soviets would respond with a nuclear attack against the United States. Given the weak Soviet military position, "we didn't believe that the Politburo would authorize the launch of one of those warheads" from Cuba or that any "sane political leader under those circumstances" would do so even in the event of a military attack from the U.S. But as he further explained in an interview,

> a Cuban sergeant or a Soviet second lieutenant under that tremendous pressure without orders would launch a warhead against one of the metropolitan areas or several warheads. And in that event millions of Americans would be killed. And no responsible U.S. President, and no responsible U.S. Secretary of Defense would put his nation at risk under those circum[stances] if he could possibly avoid it. And we were seeking to avoid it. We had avoided it up to that point. The question was, could we continue to avoid it? That was not clear.[8]

Khrushchev shared the same concerns. The shoot-down of the U-2 by a Soviet SAM brought the matter to a head for him. He mistakenly believed Castro was directly responsible for the SAM attack. According to Ellsberg, the actual chain of events was largely outside the control of Khrushchev, Castro, and the senior commanders of the Cuban and Soviet forces.

The Americans were conducting low-level reconnaissance missions, and Khrushchev had urged the Cubans not to fire at them.

They had refrained from doing so—until Saturday the 27th. Castro, believing an American invasion was about to begin, ordered his antiaircraft batteries to fire on the low-flying American planes. Khrushchev had no control over Castro's military, something Castro himself confirmed in 1984: "It was we who gave the order to fire against the low-level flights. . . . We had simply presented our view-point to [the Soviets], our opposition to low-level flights, and we ordered our batteries to fire on them."[9]

What Castro could not have predicted was the response of the Soviet field commanders when they heard firing by Cuban anti-aircraft batteries. The Soviet field officers in charge of the SAMs in Cuba were under strict orders not to shoot down American U-2 planes flying over Cuba without the authorization of their top commander, General Issa Pliyev. But one of the Soviet commanders in charge of a battery of SAMs detected a high-altitude American U-2 plane at about the same time he heard the Cuban gunners firing at the low-flying reconnaissance planes. The Cubans had never done such a thing before, and the Soviet commander thought the Cuban gunners were responding to an American invasion. He could not reach General Pliyev, and so he authorized the attack against the U-2.[10]

Although Nikita Khrushchev did not know exactly how it had happened, he did know that he had lost control over the military situation in Cuba. His son Sergei recalled when his father learned of the shoot-down: "It was at that very moment—not before or after—that Father felt the situation was slipping out of his control," and "as Father said later, that was the moment when he felt instinctively that the [ballistic] missiles had to be removed, that disaster loomed. Real disaster."[11]

Alarmed by the news that the U-2 plane had been shot down by his own military, Khrushchev and his colleagues composed the proposal that included only the noninvasion demand. This was the message that was sent on Friday. By Saturday the Russians had decided the warning they'd received about an American invasion was a false alarm, and they sent another message that included the demand to remove the missiles from Turkey.

When the Americans learned on Saturday afternoon that the U-2 plane had been shot down by a Soviet air defense missile, the ExComm assumed the Soviets were hardening their position and a peaceful resolution of the situation was much less likely. Then came the Soviet's Sunday morning broadcast agreeing to withdraw their missiles. On the surface, this sequence of events reinforced the idea that the blockade and the threats of invasion were all it took for Khrushchev to fold his cards and go home. The Russian message gave birth to what Thomas Blanton, executive director of the National Security Archive at George Washington University in Washington, D.C., called "the myth of calibrated brinksmanship"—"the belief that if you stand tough you win, and that nuclear superiority makes the difference in moments of crisis."[12]

The reality was more complex and far more frightening. In the evening of Saturday, October 27, Robert Kennedy delivered an ultimatum to the Soviet ambassador Anatoly Dobrynin: The Soviet Union must agree to remove the missiles within forty-eight hours or the United States would remove them by military force. The ultimatum was coupled with a counterproposal that if the Soviets complied, the United States would publicly accede to the noninvasion pledge and remove the missiles from Turkey within five months. But it would do the latter only if the Soviets agreed to keep that part of the agreement secret.[13]

At the Sunday morning meeting with the Presidium, Khrushchev announced he intended to accept President Kennedy's original offer, before he received the report of Robert Kennedy's warning and offer to Dobrynin. At that point, Khrushchev could have changed course and at least accepted RFK's offer. Moreover, there was no urgency since the Americans had allowed as much as forty-eight hours for a decision. Yet he followed through with his original concession message to Washington. Why?

Ellsberg later was able to talk with Fyodor Burlatsky, Khrushchev's speechwriter, about the events of that day.

"They were very, very nervous at this time [Burlatsky speaking of the drafters of the October 28 message, with whom he had been in close touch]. This letter was not drafted in the Kremlin, nor in the Politburo. It was drafted at Khrushchev's dacha, by a very small group. As soon as it was done, they ran it to the radio station. That is to say, they sent it by car, very fast. . . . When it arrived, the manager of the station himself ran down the steps, snatched the message from the hands of the man in the car, and ran up the steps to broadcast it immediately." Burlatsky didn't know, he said, why they seemed in such a hurry.[14]

So why were they in such a hurry?

In 1964 Ellsberg was able to interview Robert Kennedy as part of a "highly classified interagency study . . . of communication between governments in nuclear crises." RFK told him details of the Saturday night meeting with Ambassador Dobrynin that were not in his memoirs. He warned Dobrynin of the serious implications of the downing of the American reconnaissance plane.[15]

You have drawn first blood, and that's a very serious matter. . . . I said the president had decided against advice—strongly from the military, but not only the military—not to respond militarily to that attack, but [Dobrynin] should know that if another plane was shot at, we would shoot back [and] if one more plane was shot at, we wouldn't just attack the site that had fired at it; we would take out all the SAMs and antiaircraft and probably all the missiles. And that would almost surely be followed by an invasion.[16]

Robert Kennedy gave Dobrynin the deadline of forty-eight hours with a caveat: "Unless they shot at a plane sooner, in which case we would go right away."[17]

The problem for Khrushchev was that he didn't have firm control of the military forces in Cuba. The SAM attack against the U-2 plane had been done against his explicit orders. He couldn't be absolutely certain that it wouldn't happen again, and he had no control over the Cuban antiaircraft batteries. Khrushchev chose to end the confrontation as soon as he possibly could rather than face heavy losses and the possibility of a much wider conflict, including a nuclear one.

Only in 1992, at a conference of American, Soviet, and Cuban participants in the crisis, did it become known that about 100 tactical nuclear weapons had been deployed in Cuba. These smaller weapons were intended for use on the battlefield during an invasion by American forces; they could not reach American territory. Initially the Soviet commanders in Cuba had the authority to use them, although that authority was withdrawn.[18] But as the attack on the U-2 plane made clear, there was no assurance that the local commanders would refrain from using nuclear weapons against an American invasion—or what they thought was an American invasion.

To make matters still worse, the United States believed there were 8,000 to 10,000 Soviet troops in Cuba, while the actual number was later revealed to have been 42,000. As a result, an invasion by American troops would have been much more difficult than anticipated. The intense battle that would have ensued would have made the use of the tactical nuclear weapons all the more likely.[19] Robert McNamara, one of the attendees at the conference, said,

> We don't need to speculate what would have happened. It would have been an *absolute disaster* [italics in the original] for the world. . . . No one should believe that a U.S. force could

have been attacked by tactical nuclear warheads without responding with nuclear warheads. And where would it have ended? In utter disaster."[20]

Neither Kennedy nor Khrushchev knew about another chain of events that could have easily led to global nuclear war if it hadn't been for the fortuitous presence of one man on a Soviet submarine.

The submarine in question was one of four the Russians had sent to the waters near Cuba as part of their effort to install the missiles. When the Americans set up their blockade, they assumed the Russians might send submarines, so the U.S. sent an anti-submarine task force to the area with orders to harass the submarines into surfacing but not to attempt to destroy them.

They also sent a message to Moscow informing them that the anti-submarine groups would be using "signaling" depth charges strong enough to be felt by their targets but not strong enough to inflict serious damage. Whether this information reached senior Soviet officials is unclear. What is clear is that none of the submarine commanders knew about any of this. In addition, the Americans did not know that along with its conventional armament, each of the four Soviet submarines was equipped with one nuclear-tipped torpedo with roughly the power of the atomic bomb dropped on Hiroshima.[21]

The best-known instance in which American anti-submarine ships confronted a Soviet submarine during the blockade involved a submarine the Americans designated *B-59*.

Under continual harassment by the American navy's anti-submarine ships, the Soviet submarines were unable to surface or snorkel for days at a time. As a result, their batteries ran down, leaving them unable to keep fresh, cool air circulating. The temperature inside the submarines began to soar and carbon dioxide rose to dangerous levels.[22]

Then, the submarine was shaken by the American signaling

depth charges that the captain and crew took for an actual attack. Vadim Orlov, a signals intelligence officer aboard the submarine, described what happened as submarine commander Valentin Savitsky tried to engineer an escape while the American ships "surrounded us and started to tighten the circle . . . dropping depth charges. They exploded right next to the hull. It felt like you were sitting in a metal barrel, which somebody is constantly blasting with a sledgehammer."[23]

> The temperature was . . . up to [140 degrees]. The level of CO_2 in the air reached a critical practically deadly for people mark. One [of] the duty officers fainted and fell down. The[n] another one followed, then the third one. . . . They were falling like dominoes. . . . The Americans hit us with something stronger. . . . We thought—that's it—the end.[24]

Savitsky, who had not been able to establish communications with his superiors, ordered the nuclear torpedo to be readied for use. "We're going to blast them now! We will die, but we will sink them all—we will not disgrace our Navy!" But the torpedo was not fired. Ordinarily, two officers were required to agree to the firing of the nuclear torpedo, Savitsky and the ship's political officer. They both agreed. But it so happened a third officer was on board, Vasili Arkhipov, who was chief of staff to the brigade and the same rank as Savitsky. Although he was technically second in command to Savitsky, because of his higher command level, Arkhipov's agreement was also necessary. He withheld it on the grounds that Moscow had not authorized it.[25]

Ellsberg points out that "since no submarines known to be in the region were believed to carry nuclear warheads," American officials would have concluded the cause of the nuclear blast "would have been a medium-range missile from Cuba whose launch had not been detected." President Kennedy had already announced that the United States would respond to such an event with a full-scale nuclear attack against the Soviet Union.[26]

There was another incident that occurred the very same day that could have triggered a nuclear war, one that happened four thousand miles away. The pilot of an American U-2 reconnaissance plane from Alaska lost his bearings and ended up in Russian airspace. Low on fuel, he reversed course and began gliding back toward the United States. He didn't know Soviet MiG fighters were pursuing him.[27]

The Alaskan Air Command did know about the MiGs and scrambled to launch its own fighter planes to protect the U-2. The only armaments the American planes had were nuclear air-to-air missiles. Luckily the U-2 coasted to safety before the MiGs reached him.[28] Given what was happening in Cuba, the Russians could easily have interpreted the presence of the U-2 over their country as an opening move for a nuclear attack. Indeed, when Secretary of Defense McNamara learned this incident was underway, he left the Pentagon meeting "yelling hysterically 'this means war with the Soviet Union.'"[29]

Many of these incidents are reminiscent of what has sometimes been called the "fog of war": Events unfold in unexpected ways, often beyond the knowledge or reach of those who are ostensibly in command. Subordinates are unable to contact their commanders and so take action on their own based on their limited knowledge of the broader situation. Meanwhile, the generals may act on faulty intelligence or false assumptions about the enemy's strategy.

Examples of this "fog of war" from the Cuban Missile Crisis include a Soviet SAM missile commander assuming the antiaircraft fire he heard from his Cuban counterparts was a response to an American attack; American antisubmarine commanders carrying out orders that almost certainly would have been very different if their superiors had known the Soviet submarines were carrying nuclear weapons; and the Pentagon planning to invade

Cuba without knowing about the presence of Soviet tactical nuclear weapons on the island.

No amount of planning or intelligence can account for these kinds of unexpected contingencies. The situation is succinctly described by the old doggerel: "For want of a nail the shoe was lost/ For want of a shoe the horse was lost . . . /For want of a battle the kingdom was lost/All for the want of a horseshoe nail." In the Cuban case, there was an extra "nail" in the form of an additional officer in a Soviet submarine who prevented a war that all would have lost.

In a war, each side knows the intentions of the other side: to attack whenever possible. But when military forces are brought to the edge of conflict under a situation of "neither war, nor peace," each side must constantly judge the intentions of the other. What seems like the beginning of a massive invasion may only be the actions of an individual commander who has been accidentally cut off from his superiors; what appears like a deadly attack against a submarine may not be so. Under such circumstances, the chances for a fatal miscalculation may be even greater than they might be in actual war. We have been more than fortunate that a few people made the right decision at a fateful moment.

Yet perhaps the person most responsible for helping the world escape relatively unscathed from the most dangerous incident of the Cold War was Nikita Khrushchev. Granted, Khrushchev's initial move of putting the missiles in Cuba was a rash miscalculation; and granted, Kennedy deserves credit for resisting the advice of his more bellicose advisors. Nonetheless, it was Khrushchev who was willing to make major concessions regardless of the political cost to his own position. As he later commented in an interview,

When I asked the military advisors if they could assure me that holding fast would not result in the death of five hundred million human beings, they looked at me as though I was out of my mind, or what was worse, a traitor. The biggest tragedy, as they saw it, was not that our country might be devastated and everything lost, but that the Chinese or the Albanians might accuse us of appeasement or weakness. So I said to myself, "To hell with these maniacs. If I can get the United States to assure me that it will not attempt to overthrow the Cuban government, I will remove the missiles." That is what happened, and now I am reviled by the Chinese and the Albanians. . . . They say I was afraid to stand up to a paper tiger. It is all such nonsense. What good would it have done me in the last hour of my life to know that though our great nation and the United States were in complete ruins, the national honor of the Soviet Union was intact?[30]

CHAPTER 12

Stumbling into Nuclear War

A dramatic confrontation in which one side failed to "blink" was not the only way a nuclear war could start. Instead, small changes to what one what country believes is a routine military procedure—one its adversary has long recognized as such—could be interpreted as a mortal threat. That is what happened in November of 1983. Gorbachev later described the atmosphere at the time: "Never, perhaps, in the postwar decades has the situation in the world been as explosive . . . as in the first half of the eighties."[1]

That was the environment under which NATO began its annual war simulation exercises. The NATO war simulation for that year, called Able Archer 83, included some departures from past exercises. According to documents that were declassified in the mid 1980s, those changes "may have inadvertently placed [U.S.] relations with the Soviet Union on a hair trigger" during the exercise.[2]

Able Archer was the name of an annual exercise that had been taking place for several years. Unfortunately, the 1983 version included some new features the Soviets found particularly alarming. The exercise included "new command, control, and communications procedures for authorizing use of nuclear weapons."[3] U.S. aircraft "practiced the nuclear warhead handling procedures, including taxiing out of hangars carrying realistic-looking dummy warheads."[4]

The Soviets appear to have responded by initiating a "force-wide" alert during Able Archer 83. The U.S. had "not seen a 'force-wide' Soviet alert since World War II."[5] U.S. intelligence reports also concluded that the "war scare was an expression of a genuine belief on the part of Soviet leaders that [the] US was planning a nuclear first strike, causing Sov[iet] military to prepare for this eventuality, for example by readying forces for a Sov[iet] preemptive strike."[6]

Soviet armed forces were moving to high alert, but "officers acted correctly out of instinct, not informed guidance."[7] Caspar Weinberger agreed the Soviet reaction was not entirely unwarranted: "The difference between a realistic exercise or maneuver and what could be preparations for an attack, that line is sometimes quite blurred."[8]

U.S. intelligence officials attempted to bury the knowledge of the Soviet alert by sending the reports "to languish in an annex . . . that was unintended for policymakers' eyes" until the senior officer who had been involved in the incident sent the intelligence officials a "'parting shot' before retirement . . . [with] a letter 'outlining his disquiet over the inadequate treatment of the Soviet war scare.'"[9]

A few weeks after Able Archer 83, Reagan wrote in his diary that the Soviets were "paranoid about being attacked." Later, after being more fully briefed on what had happened, Reagan replied: "I don't see how they could believe that—but it's something to think about."[10]

Fortunately, "the military officers in charge of the Able Archer exercise minimized this risk" with a "fortuitous" decision to do "nothing in the face of evidence that parts of the Soviet armed forces were moving to an unusual level of alert."[11] Caspar Weinberger agreed the Soviet reaction was not entirely unwarranted: "The difference between a realistic exercise or maneuver and what could be preparations for an attack, that line is sometimes quite blurred."[12]

CHAPTER 13

Star Wars

O n March 23, 1983, President Ronald Reagan gave a speech in support of his administration's defense budget for the next fiscal year. The Defense Department had provided Reagan with a draft. But he surprised everyone in his own administration except for a few of his closest staff members when he deviated from the speech that had been prepared for him.[1]

He did invoke the language that was so often used in support of increased military funding: he said America was suffering from a "decade of neglecting our military forces," during which "the Soviets have built up a massive arsenal of new strategic nuclear weapons—weapons that can strike directly at the United States" and that they were using their increased strength to spread "their military influence in ways that can directly challenge our vital interests and those of our allies."[2] Reagan then went on to point out that the threat of nuclear war made it "necessary to rely on the specter of retaliation, on mutual threat." That, he said, was "a sad commentary on the human condition. Wouldn't it be better to save lives than to avenge them?"

His surprise in the defense budget speech was his claim that it was now possible to develop systems that "could intercept and destroy strategic ballistic missiles before they reached our own soil or that of our allies." He called "upon the scientific community in our country, those who gave us nuclear weapons, to turn their great talents now to the cause of mankind and world peace, to give us the means of rendering these weapons impotent and obsolete."[3]

Frances FitzGerald noted in her expansive account of the Strategic Defense Initiative (SDI):

[The] President's call for a program to make ballistic missiles obsolete appalled defense experts in and out of the administration. The Joint Chiefs were stunned by the precipitous action and the sweeping language. The chief technical experts in the Pentagon were furious. According to witnesses, Richard DeLauer, the undersecretary of defense for research and engineering, "went ballistic" and asked how nuclear policy could be the subject of such a "half-baked political travesty."[4]

Congressional Democrats mocked the speech. Democratic senator Edward Markey of Massachusetts said Reagan wanted to create a "pin-ball outer-space war between the Force of Evil and the Force of Good." Meanwhile, most of the Republicans in Congress chose silence as their safest option.

The press was equally scathing. *Newsweek* labeled the proposal "Star Wars." *Time* magazine's cover showed Reagan with Buck Rogers weaponry on its cover and described the president's proposal as a "video-game vision" while suggesting it was also "partly a political ploy to change the context of the debate over defense spending." The *New York Times* called the idea "a pipe dream, a projection of fantasy in policy."[5]

The record shows that *Time* magazine and the *New York Times* were both correct: Reagan's proposal was a political ploy, and it was also a projection of fantasy into policy. Reagan himself often behaved as if politics was almost entirely an exercise in fantasy. For those who worked most closely with him, Reagan seemed to treat his job as president in much the same way as he did his career as an actor. Every morning his chief of staff handed him his daily schedule, which he followed almost without fail. Donald Regan, who served as Reagan's chief of staff from 1985 to 1987, noted that Reagan treated the schedule as "something like a shooting script."[6] One White House official heard the president say, "They tell me what to do. Each morning I get a piece of paper that tells me what I do all day long." Donald Regan observed that following the schedule seemed to give Reagan a feeling of "regularity and tangible measure of accomplishment that evidently was deeply pleasing to him." FitzGerald also notes that "when he appeared at Cabinet meetings, White House aides were tempted to add directions: enter stage left, action, exit stage right."[7]

President Reagan rarely set his own policy. Instead, as Donald Regan put it, he "chose his aides and then followed their advice almost without question. . . . He listened, acquiesced, played his role and waited the for the next act to be written."[8]

This created a power vacuum that led to a great deal of bureaucratic infighting. As one senior Pentagon official observed, "The timing of meetings with Reagan is very important because everybody knows that with people he likes, the last one to see him can usually carry the day."[9]

Reagan's close advisors tried to keep the various factions away from the Oval Office out of fear that policies would keep changing depending upon who had the last word with the president. But as FitzGerald noted, "In the view of outsiders, they isolated the President, kept like a bird in a gilded cage."[10]

What Reagan did do was make speeches. Reagan's first chief of staff, James Baker, observed that Reagan expected his advisors to make policies consistent with his speeches, and Reagan would then follow up by selling them to the public.[11]

In that sense, Reagan did have a vision even if he didn't have any idea how to turn that vision into a workable reality. He spent much of the 1950s and early 1960s presenting his vision in speeches throughout the country. One associate of his during that time remembered his speech as extolling "old American values . . . like the Boy Scout code, you know, not very informative. But always lively with entertaining stories. . .. He promoted anti-Communism and the free enterprise system."[12]

Reagan denounced Medicare—then a program that provided medical care for military dependents—as "a foot in the door of a government take-over of all medicine"; called for Social Security to be made voluntary; and questioned almost every social program enacted since the New Deal. Later, Reagan wrote: "I wasn't just making speeches—I was preaching a sermon."[13]

Reagan was by no means an analytical thinker. But he did have a photographic memory,[14] a talent that served him well when learning movie scripts and also when looking for bits and pieces of information he could use to bolster his arguments. FitzGerald described his method:

> He picked up pieces of information like a magpie without concern for the provenance. He valued every piece equally, and there was no piece that could be not replaced by another that would illustrate his point just as well. . . . The method Reagan used was not deductive; it was not inductive either, for the conclusions came before the evidence. . . . That is, his assumptions and moral precepts served as aggregation devices for anecdotes and bits of information that he would store away for future use—and anything that did not adhere to them would simply pass him by. Just as in a sermon, Reagan began with a lesson and then worked to present it as convincingly as possible.[15]

A similar process seems to have been behind Reagan's advocacy of a space-based defense against ballistic missiles. Martin Anderson, an economist at the Hoover Institution and later a high-level domestic policy advisor in the Reagan administration, described a visit to the North American Aerospace Defense Command (NORAD) he had helped arrange for Reagan in July 1979, during the early stages of Reagan's presidential campaign.

Anderson traveled with Reagan to the NORAD base located inside Cheyenne Mountain, Colorado. In his account of the visit, Anderson described "a vast underground city . . . carved deep into the granite core" of the mountain from which dozens of people monitored screens that displayed information coming in from a worldwide network designed to detect "the first sign of a nuclear attack." However, the base commander, General James Hill, explained they could only track the trajectory of incoming missiles. There was nothing they could do to stop even a single one of them.[16]

Anderson recalled how on the way home Reagan mused, "We have spent all that money and have all that equipment, and there is nothing we can do to prevent a nuclear missile from hitting us." A little later Reagan declared, "We should have some way of defending ourselves against nuclear missiles." Anderson goes on to imply that a memo he wrote to Reagan shortly after the visit to NORAD may have led Reagan to favor the adoption of a "protective missile system." Such a system, Anderson wrote, "is probably fundamentally far more appealing to the American people than the questionable satisfaction of knowing that those who initiated an attack against us were also blown away," and that "there have apparently been striking advances in missile technology . . . that would make such a system technically possible."[17]

Anderson claimed Reagan wanted to incorporate the idea of missile defense into his campaign, but his political advisors objected that "there was no way Reagan could discuss radical changes in traditional nuclear weapons policy without leaving himself wide open to demagogic attacks from his Democratic opponent."[18]

Some of the language he used in interviews with the press not long after the "Star Wars" speech suggests that the NORAD trip may have simply reinforced notions about nuclear war that Reagan already had. In the speech he said, "It's inconceivable to me that we can go on thinking down the future, not only for ourselves and our lifetime but for other generations, that the great nations of the world will sit here, like people facing themselves across a table [sic], each with a cocked gun and no one knowing whether someone must tighten their finger on the trigger."[19] A few days later he added, "To look down to an endless future with both of us sitting here with these horrible missiles aimed at each other and the only thing preventing a holocaust is just so long as no one pulls the trigger—this is unthinkable."[20]

FitzGerald points out that his comments to the reporters were "made up of lines from Reagan's previous speeches— from the speeches designed to show that he was not a nuclear warmonger. . . . [T]he notion of the judgment of future generations came from his much-applauded speech at the 1976 Republican convention."[21]

Reagan's "magpie" sensibilities, always on the alert for a useful anecdote or turn of phrase, might have also been at work. His framing of the idea resembled ideas from at least two movies. In one of them, a 1940 film called *Murder in the Air*, Reagan played a secret agent who stops enemy agents from stealing the secrets of the "inertia projector," a ray gun that could destroy all enemy planes as they flew through the air. In the film, a navy admiral claims the weapon "not only makes the United States invincible in war but, in doing so, promises to become the greatest force for world peace ever discovered."

Then there was Alfred Hitchcock's 1966 film, *Torn Curtain*, in which Paul Newman plays an American agent who declares that with an antimissile missile "we will produce a defensive weapon that will make all nuclear weapons obsolete, and thereby abolish the terror of nuclear warfare." FitzGerald notes that "Reagan's own aides were struck by the similarity of the language to that of Reagan's speech."[22]

However, there were other more contemporary influences that probably also affected Reagan's thinking in the years leading up to his Star Wars speech. As early as 1979 a small group of politicians, scientists, and advisors began calling for a space-based antiballistic missile system that could shoot down enemy missiles before they reached the United States. They offered firm but largely illusory promises that the technology for creating such a system was already available and we needed only to summon the will to make use of it.

The first person to call Reagan's attention to the idea was Senator Malcolm Wallop of Montana, who sent Reagan the draft of an article he had written for *Strategic Review*, a conservative journal, in which he claimed technology was already available that could "conceivably destroy a whole fleet of ballistic missiles" with just two dozen space-based laser weapons.[23]

In fact, Wallop did not write the *Strategic Review* article himself. It was drafted for him by one of his staff members, Angelo Codevilla, who had, in turn, picked up the idea from an aerospace engineer at Lockheed. Wallop and Codevilla had little success in getting support from the Defense Department for such a project beyond a willingness to undertake some research.[24]

Another key figure in this story is Lieutenant General Daniel Graham, who had been the director of the Defense Intelligence Agency from 1974 to 1976. He served as Reagan's military advisor during his 1980 presidential campaign and briefed him on the idea of a space-based missile system in February of that year. In 1981 he published his own ideas in the *Strategic Review*. The next year he helped make the concept better known, at least among political conservatives, with his book—*High Frontier: A New National Strategy*. The Heritage Foundation helped ensure that the army and air force conducted full evaluations of his missile defense proposal.[25]

Reagan made only fleeting public references to Star Wars from late 1983 to January 1985. The reason had to do with tactical considerations related to his election campaign. In September of 1983 polling indicated that although the American people approved of Reagan's domestic policy, they did not approve of his foreign policy, and they were particularly nervous about his aggressive military posture.

His advisors sought to shore up his image as a statesman by sending him on a series of largely ceremonial visits to Japan, Korea, China, Ireland, Britain, and France from late 1983 into June 1984. During these visits, he dropped much of his rhetoric about the need to build up the military to counter the Communist menace. Instead, he made generic verbal gestures toward more peaceful relations with the Soviets, declaring, "Neither we nor the Soviet Union can wish away the differences between our two societies and our philosophies. But we should always remember that we have common interests. And foremost among them is to avoid war and reduce the level of arms."[26]

A White House official told the *Washington Post* in 1984 that as far as the SDI was concerned, "there was a conscious decision not to invest more in it this year, because it's an election year. . . . He's low-keyed the program." When Democrats criticized the SDI during the campaign, Reagan responded blandly that it was just a research program that might result in "a defensive weapon to defend against incoming missiles."[27]

The SDI did not completely disappear from public awareness during that period. There were articles about it in the major newspapers, and the television networks aired documentaries as well. But the Reagan campaign did what it could to keep it away from the center of attention.

That reticence promptly disappeared after the election. Almost immediately after the election results were in, Reagan claimed the Soviets would rapidly retreat from the nuclear arms race because with SDI "we've proven that it's possible to be invulnerable to such an attack." He also emphasized it in his second inaugural address, declaring once again:

Now, for decades, we and the Soviets have lived under the threat of mutual assured destruction—if either resorted to the use of nuclear weapons, the other could retaliate and destroy the one who had started it. Is there either logic or morality in believing that if one side threatens to kill tens of millions of our people our only recourse is to threaten killing tens of millions of theirs?

I have approved a research program to find, if we can, a security shield that would destroy nuclear missiles before they reach their target. It wouldn't kill people; it would destroy weapons. It wouldn't militarize space; it would help demilitarize the arsenals of Earth.[28]

FitzGerald describes the response of administration officials to Reagan's renewed promise of a security shield against nuclear missiles:

In the months after Reagan's reelection administration officials, including those most disturbed by Reagan's 1983 speech, publicly professed faith in SDI in a manner that reminded former Deputy Secretary of State George Ball of the mass conversion decreed by King Ethelbert of Kent in the sixth century. High officials spoke of "the President's vision" and vowed fealty to Reagan's "ultimate goal." [Secretary of Defense] Caspar Weinberger went so far as to say that SDI was "the only thing that offers any real hope to the world."[29]

Undersecretary of Defense Fred Iklé told the Senate Armed Services Committee it was official Defense Department policy that "the Strategic Defense Initiative is not an optional program, at the margin of the defense effort. It's central, at the very core of our long-term policy for reducing the risk of nuclear war."[30]

The effusive comments by Reagan and senior officials, along with requests for sharply increased funding, helped return Star Wars to public awareness. They also led to a public controversy between scientists working on the SDI and outside technical experts that became known as the "science wars."[31]

The basic idea behind the proposals was for a multilayered system: The first layer would consist of systems that could attack missiles during their "boost phase" as they left their launch sites and destroy them using lasers, particle beams, "smart rocks," and "smart pebbles," tiny missiles which could home in on big enemy ballistic missiles and destroy them on impact. The second layer would attack the surviving enemy missiles during the "post-boost" phase in which the missiles maneuver to release several independently targeted warheads and decoys. This layer would use the same technology as the first. The third layer would consist of ground-launched interceptor missiles to destroy any surviving warheads as they descended toward their target.[32]

The press helped make the science wars a national issue. The *New York Times* and the *Washington Post* both ran multipart series describing the SDI. Stories and opinion pieces appeared frequently in other newspapers around the country. The American public and Congress became familiar with discussions of laser weapons and the "boost phase" of nuclear-tipped ICBMs. They also learned the price tag for the SDI might be as high as a trillion dollars—and still leave the United States vulnerable to a nuclear attack.[33]

One of the flashpoints for the controversy was a report completed in 1984 at the request of Congress by a Harvard professor and former Defense Department analyst who had full access to the classified information associated with the SDI. He concluded that the likelihood that such a system could protect the American public was "so remote that it should not serve as the basis of public expectations of national policy on ballistic missile defense." A physicist from Los Alamos who supported the SDI program countered that the congressional report was "full of technical errors, unsubstantiated assumptions, and conclusions that are inconsistent with the body of the report" and went on to charge the Harvard professor of being politically biased.[34]

One of the core criticisms of SDI was that it would be impractical even if the futuristic technologies of smart rocks, lasers, and superfast orbiting computers could actually be developed. The problem was that each missile could contain at least ten individually targeted warheads plus hundreds of decoys and clouds of radar-confusing chaff. If a thousand missiles with multiple warheads reached space, the SDI system would have to locate and destroy ten thousand warheads within a "threat cloud" of hundreds of thousands of other objects during the twenty minutes it would take for the warheads to arrive at their targets. Such capabilities were completely beyond any known technology.

Therefore, the SDI would have to destroy the two thousand missiles the Soviets had during their three- to five-minute boost phase before they reached orbit and could release their individually targeted warheads. In order to do so, many of the SDI weapons would have to be permanently positioned in orbit directly over the Soviet Union. However, in that case critics pointed out, the Soviets could easily attack the SDI weapons orbiting over their territory with "space mines, anti-satellite weapons or nuclear bursts at high altitudes" before launching their missile attack against the United States itself. Secretary Weinberger publicly dismissed these concerns saying "many scientists have said a great many things that have proven to be wrong once the work has been done" and that the critics were "traditional thinkers" who were "congenitally opposed to new ideas."[35]

Despite the administration's reticence concerning the SDI in an election year, the program became the focus of hearings before the Senate Foreign Relations Committee in 1984. In those hearings administration officials admitted that in order to destroy enemy missiles during the boost phase, the system's computers would have to respond before there was any time for a human decision. Senator and former astronaut John Glenn, who attended the hearing, commented, "I have followed all the different types of lasers, high-velocity kinetic weapons, particles and such for fifteen or eighteen years now. . . . I have supported laser research and particle beam research. . . . But it seemed to me, and it seemed to me ever since the President talked about this, that what we are talking about is something that has not yet been invented. . . . I cannot believe we are . . . just assuming that the basic physics of this thing works."[36]

Administration officials dismissed these concerns. Secretary Weinberger said, "Many scientists said a few years ago that we couldn't ever reach the moon." General James Abrahamson, the Pentagon director of research for SDI, declared, "I don't think anything in this country is technically impossible. We have a nation which indeed can produce miracles."[37]

Indeed, miracles were the stock-in-trade of Ronald Reagan and his administration. As his science advisor George Keyworth explained, "It was of little value to the Administration, at least in policy advisory positions, to have people who do not share the Administration's view." According to Keyworth, Reagan was not interested in practical concerns: "He knows exactly where he wants to go, but couldn't care less about how to get there. . . . The President doesn't care about wavelengths and things like that."[38]

As Daniel Ellsberg's account of nuclear war planning shows, the reality that exists within the walls of bureaucracy is often quite different from the reality beyond them. The SDI was no exception. Various players in the White House, the Pentagon, and Congress used it to their advantage in factional disputes. For some, the issue was budgets; for others, it was disarmament policy; for still others, it was securing American missiles against a Soviet first strike.

What the SDI did not do was make Americans more secure from nuclear annihilation. As an article in the *Bulletin of the Atomic*

Scientists put it, "In the end, the Strategic Defense Initiative proved to be a major distraction that undermined nuclear disarmament efforts every step of the way."[39]

What the SDI did do was provide useful leverage for undercutting a popular political movement for disarmament that had arisen in 1980: the Nuclear Freeze campaign. This campaign called for the United States and the Soviet Union to halt "the testing, production and deployment of nuclear weapons and of missiles and new aircraft designed primarily to deliver nuclear weapons." The resolution went on to lay out in some detail how the initial stages of the freeze could have been implemented under existing nuclear weapons agreements, and it described some of the specific weapons systems and technologies on each side that would come under a freeze agreement.[40]

Backed by sixty-nine Catholic bishops as well as several major Protestant denominations, the movement soon had adherents across the country. During this time, a number of books were published on nuclear war, most notably Jonathan Schell's *The Fate of the Earth*, which gave a detailed description of what would happen to the country in the event of a nuclear war. In March 1982, bipartisan resolutions calling for a freeze were introduced in both the House of Representatives and the Senate. The bill in the House had 115 cosponsors.[41]

Senior members of the Reagan administration denounced the proposals as "bad defense and security policy" and "harmful to our security and that of our allies" and declared that it would "play entirely into the hands of the Soviet Union." Reagan himself voiced his opposition because "on balance the Soviet Union does have a definite measure of superiority."[42] David Gergen, White House communications director at the time, recalled, "There was a widespread view in the administration that the freeze was a dagger pointed at the heart of the administration's defense program."[43]

By the summer of 1982, nationwide polls showed public support for a nuclear freeze at over 70 percent. In the fall of that year, "freeze referenda appeared on the ballot in 10 states, the District of Columbia, and 37 cities and counties around the nation, voters delivered a victory to the freeze campaign in nine of the states and in all but three localities. Covering about one-third of the U.S. electorate, this was the largest referendum on a single issue in U.S. history."[44]

That fall the National Council of Catholic Bishops released the draft of a proposed pastoral letter to be sent to the fifty-one million Catholics in the United States condemning "the arms race, war-fighting doctrines and first-strike weapons." By December, twenty-five states and over "eight hundred city and county councils and town meetings had passed freeze referenda."[45] In May of 1983, the House of Representatives passed a nuclear freeze resolution by a vote of 278 to 149.[46]

The language Reagan used in his second inaugural speech to describe the SDI was carefully calibrated based on polling data. It was just part of what an internal planning memorandum from December of 1984 described as a "public affairs blitz" to "carry the gospel" of the SDI into major media markets. The message was that the United States was taking the "moral high ground" by seeking to defend itself from a "balance of terror."[47]

The public affairs blitz "appropriated the rhetoric of the anti-nuclear movement" and used it to justify the SDI. Once it had successfully done so, the Nuclear Freeze "melted away."[48] Even cogent critiques that exposed the exaggerated claims for the effectiveness of Star Wars had the opposite of their intended effects: Extended technical discussions questioning the virtues of orbiting computers, high-powered lasers, "smart rocks," and so forth led people to believe we could build such things if only we put our minds to it. Just as General Abrahamson said, America was "a nation which indeed can produce miracles" and it was un-American to claim otherwise.

What this carefully crafted rhetoric hid from the public was something virtually every government official except possibly Reagan fully understood: Even if the technology of the SDI could be developed, it would never offer a reliable umbrella against a full-scale nuclear attack. The reason for this was simple arithmetic. If the SDI stopped 99 percent of the 10,000 nuclear warheads headed toward the United States, that would still leave 100 missiles getting through—more than enough to devastate the country. Nothing less than 99.9 percent would do. Even the SDI's most ardent advocates conceded that it was unlikely that any defensive system could be that effective.[49]

A Defense Department study confirmed that "nearly leak-proof defenses are required to provide a high level of protection for the population" and that such defenses "may prove to be unattainable." Even Daniel Graham's 1982 position paper from the *High Frontier* did not claim the system would protect the American people from a Soviet nuclear attack. The chief scientist in charge of SDI told a journalist, "Nobody believes in 100 percent anything that's ever worked on military systems." In fact, "no official administration document and no administration expert speaking under oath ever claimed" that SDI could protect the American people.[50]

For example, when asked how, after spending a trillion dollars on antimissile defenses, he would explain to the American people that they were still not protected from a nuclear attack, General Abrahamson's response was typical: "I do not believe that this is what we have ever really said. . . . It is a defense deterrent that we are talking about . . . to prevent them from being able to hit your military capability." Franklin Miller, the director of the Office of Strategic Forces Policy at the Pentagon, told Congress during the hearings of 1984 the same thing.[51]

Through all of this, the president kept on giving speeches about making Americans safe from nuclear weapons. But his message was anything but consistent. In an election-day interview, he talked as though an effective SDI system already existed. In a January 1985 news conference, SDI was once again just a research program. Sometimes he talked of the protection SDI might provide as his "hope" or "dream." Yet in February of 1985, he told the *Wall Street Journal*,

> Oh, I've never asked for 100 percent. That would be a fine goal; but you can have a most effective defensive weapon even if it isn't 100 percent. Because what you would have is that the other fellow would have the knowledge that if they launched a first strike, that it might be such that not enough of their missiles would get through, and in return we could launch a retaliatory strike.[52]

FitzGerald suggests Reagan may not have really believed any of these statements. "After all, Reagan said one thing in his speeches and another to journalists with total aplomb, and given his lack of interest in most matters of policy, it is conceivable that he had no beliefs on the subject at all."[53] She also suggests that the different positions he took served the interests of different elements in the bureaucracy. In other words, his behavior reflected the White House dynamics, whereby what Reagan said depended upon which of his advisors was able to get in the last word with him.

In 1985 Congress allocated three billion dollars for the SDI program. The Democrats were not happy about this decision, but the politics of the issue had passed the point of rational debate. Tom Foley, a Democratic congressman from Washington, lamented, "We couldn't argue the counter-intuitive." FitzGerald summed up the situation nicely: "SDI was surely the first military program the Congress had . . . voted for knowing full well that what the public expected from it could not possibly be achieved."[54]

CHAPTER 14

Star Wars Goes Global

A lthough it was a virtual certainty that the Strategic Defense Initiative would never completely protect the American people from a nuclear attack, it proved to be a bureaucratic Swiss Army knife—a tool with many functions that different players within the system could employ for their own ends. Ironically, this proved to be the case in the Soviet Union as well as in the United States.

Much of the bureaucratic infighting over the SDI was part of a broader conflict between Secretary of State George Shultz and Secretary of Defense Caspar Weinberger. Shultz strongly favored arms control negotiations; Weinberger believed the Soviet Union was an implacable enemy and negotiations were both futile and dangerous. Reagan would make conciliatory gestures toward one side or the other but took no action to resolve the conflict. Infighting between the Departments of Defense and State continued unabated.[1]

Like General Abrahamson, Caspar Weinberger viewed the SDI as something that, as Weinberger put it, allowed for "defense of the offensive deterrent forces, which of course we still have to maintain."[2] He also backed the position of his Assistant Secretary of Defense for Global Strategic Affairs, Richard Perle. Although Perle had earlier ridiculed the concepts behind the SDI as "the product of millions of American teenagers putting quarters into video machines," he changed his stance once he saw that the SDI could be used, not only to thwart Shultz's efforts at negotiations, but also to undermine existing arms control treaties.[3]

First and foremost among the latter was the Anti-Ballistic Missile (ABM) Treaty, which had been signed in 1972. With some very narrow exceptions, the ABM Treaty banned the deployment of missiles designed to destroy incoming enemy missiles. The agreement reduced the likelihood that the United States and the Soviet Union would engage in an accelerated arms race with each side building systems that could destroy enemy missiles while simultaneously developing systems that could evade or overwhelm their opponents' defenses.

However, the treaty did allow for research on such systems, presumably on the assumption that each side needed to be prepared if its counterpart broke the agreement. Perle believed the United States would benefit from an arms race between the United States and the Soviet Union. For that reason, he supported efforts to fund the development of the SDI. Such a step would destroy the ABM Treaty and undermine Shultz's plans for more extensive arms agreements with the Soviet Union. To that end, he "took to delivering reports on great progress and the promise of technical marvels to come."[4]

Meanwhile, the Soviets suggested negotiations to prevent the militarization of space. Shultz noted that the Soviets had protested that the SDI was a step toward "the development of large-scale ABM weapons," and he saw their concerns as an opportunity for the U.S. to give up space weaponry in return for a general reduction in nuclear weapons.[5]

Thus, although neither Weinberger nor Shultz believed the SDI would protect the American people from a nuclear attack, they both supported the public relations effort to convince the American people that the SDI would slow the development of nuclear weapons. Yet each of them did so with contradictory goals in mind: Weinberger, like Perle, wanted to accelerate the arms race by undermining existing arms control agreements, while Shultz hoped to slow or even end the arms race by reaching new agreements. As it turned out, both men's goals were thwarted: The SDI did nothing to further Weinberger's objectives and proved fatal for Shultz's.

The Soviet Union's political and military leadership initially interpreted Reagan's Star Wars speech of 1983 as an attempt by the United States to strengthen its own first-strike capability while weakening the Soviet Union's capacity to retaliate. They viewed the SDI as further justification for their concerns about the militarization of space, and they leveraged the publicity generated by the Star Wars speech to pursue a treaty that would ban space-based weapons.[6]

Arms control analyst Pavel Podvig also suggests that although such a ban "would have certainly affected SDI-related programs, the Soviet initiative did not appear to be a direct response to the U.S. program. Rather, it was an extension of its earlier efforts to reach a ban on space weapons." The Soviet overtures collapsed under the weight of worsening relations with the United States, especially the American deployment of intermediate-range missiles in Europe in 1983.[7]

However, as in the United States, Soviet leaders had to contend with hard-liners within their own ranks. Podvig suggests that rather than inducing the Soviet Union to move toward peace, the SDI "embolden[ed] those in the Soviet Union who defined security in confrontational terms" and that they enthusiastically seized "the opportunity to advance [their] projects."[8]

Initially Soviet defense industry leaders pushed for more funding for previously existing space-based projects that could be used to counter the SDI. Later they pushed to build an SDI of their own, despite their doubts—similar to those held by their American counterparts—about the feasibility of the underlying technology.[9]

By July 1985, the Soviet government had committed to an acceleration of its own space-based missile defense system similar to the United States' Star Wars proposal. This came as a response to the SDI and the increasingly aggressive stance by the United States, especially the open discussions among American leaders about abandoning existing arms control agreements.[10] The Soviets eventually decided that attacking a space-based missile defense system such as the SDI was cheaper and more practical than trying to build their own.[11]

Meanwhile, in November of 1985, Reagan and the new Soviet leader, Mikhail Gorbachev, met in Geneva for two days of arms control talks. Gorbachev was much younger and far more personable than his predecessors. Despite a contentious preparatory meeting with Secretary of State Shultz, Gorbachev "had long ago determined to have a cordial meeting with Reagan, no matter what the prospects for arms control."[12]

"Cordiality" seemed to have been the byword at Geneva, even though there were no meaningful negotiations during the two-day summit. Both men had prepared ahead of time by learning personal details about their counterpart. Reagan learned which was Gorbachev's favorite soccer team, while the Soviet General Secretary watched Reagan's film *King's Row* as part of his pre-summit preparations and showed an avid interest in Reagan's personal stories about such actors as Jimmy Stewart, John Wayne, and Humphrey Bogart.[13]

They did not shy away from conflict during the plenary sessions. According to Reagan's chief of staff, Donald Regan, the president and Gorbachev "went at it like taxi drivers after a fender-bender, and Reagan seemed to enjoy the give-and-take."[14]

Perhaps the most publicized event was a carefully arranged "spontaneous" invitation by Reagan for Gorbachev to join him for a private conversation at a lakeside pool house, where they discussed arms control by the fireplace accompanied only by their translators. American officials said the two leaders developed a real "personal chemistry," and that Reagan had come to respect Gorbachev. Shultz wrote that between the two men at the final ceremony, "The personal chemistry was apparent. The easy and relaxed attitude toward each other, the smiles, the sense of purpose, all showed through."[15]

Gorbachev seemed to enjoy being with Reagan; he told his advisors that for all his flaws, Reagan might be someone the Soviets could work with. However, a sense of unreality was a pervasive undercurrent at Geneva. One of his advisors wrote, "It seemed to me that everything looked like theater . . . and that in this theater there was a professional actor." On the other hand, the Soviet ambassador to the United States, Anatoly Dobrynin, remarked: "Gorbachev himself was a very good actor."[16]

The assessment that Reagan was merely making use of his acting skills at Geneva may have been too harsh. After all, Reagan seemed unable, or at least unwilling, to distinguish affability from substance. Hence, it is not surprising that, as FitzGerald reports, he "marked Geneva as the greatest moment of his presidency."[17]

Nonetheless, substance did not go entirely unaddressed at Geneva. The Soviets had already offered to reduce its store of nuclear missiles by 50 percent, but only on the condition that the United States would refrain from militarizing space.

> Gorbachev . . . went on: "You are trying to catch the firebird with technology. How can we go before the world and say we lost the chance for fifty percent reductions because we wouldn't stop research on space weapons?"
>
> "How can you defend a chance for fifty percent reductions just because you were stubborn [about a] research [program]?" Reagan replied.[18]

A year later, at an arms control summit at Reykjavík, the two leaders would discuss eliminating almost all nuclear weapons. Yet a supposed "research" project to eliminate nuclear weapons proved to be the rock on which those plans foundered.

Well before that summit, in January 1986, Gorbachev surprised American officials by proposing a sweeping arms control agreement that would eliminate nuclear weapons in three five-year stages, not only those of the United States and the Soviet Union but also those of the other nuclear powers: France, Britain, and China. The agreement would eliminate not just ballistic missiles but also tactical nuclear weapons and ban nuclear testing and exotic nonnuclear weapons such as lasers. Gorbachev's proposal also included on-site verification and the reduction of conventional forces. In the first of three five-year stages, the U.S. and the Soviet Union would reduce their strategic missiles by half and remove all of their intermediate-range missiles from Europe. In the second, the other nuclear powers, France, Britain, and China, would freeze their nuclear forces at the current level. In the third five-year stage, all other nuclear weapons including those delivered by bombers would be eliminated. Fatefully, the Soviet proposal also called for an end to the development, testing, and deployment of "space-strike weapons."[19]

Shultz believed this proposal was a useful starting point for future negotiations. On the other hand, some of his deputies feared it would result in a Europe that was neutral in the conflict between the U.S. and the Soviets and thus lead to the end of NATO. Meanwhile, in the Defense Department, Richard Perle claimed Gorbachev's offer was pure propaganda.[20] (Ironically, in 1981 Perle himself had advocated a "zero option" as a propaganda ploy for the then upcoming arms control negotiations.[21]) Reagan replied to Gorbachev with a handwritten letter welcoming his disarmament proposal but offering almost nothing that could serve as a basis for further negotiations.[22]

The disarmament plan was not Gorbachev's only unexpected move. In late February 1986, the Soviet Communist Party began its Twenty-Seventh Congress. The Congress was held every five years to reevaluate its "'general line'" of policy and choose the membership of its Central Committee.

Gorbachev had initially intended to announce his disarmament plan in his speech to the Congress. But after consulting with other members of the leadership, he decided to publish the plan before he gave the speech so that it would be understood to be an official act of the Soviet government rather than a policy adopted by the Communist Party.

What he did discuss in his speech to Congress was at least as surprising. After making the expected references to the exploitive nature of capitalism, Gorbachev suggested that there are contradictions "on a global scale, affecting the very foundations of the existence of civilization," including the "pollution of the environment, the air, the ocean and the depletion of natural resources." Addressing these problems would require "cooperation on a worldwide scale [and] . . . close and constructive joint action by a majority of countries."[23]

Perhaps the most remarkable part of his speech was a reference to a comment Ronald Reagan had made at Geneva:

> The U.S. President once said that if our planet were threatened by a landing from another planet, the U.S.S.R. and the U.S.A. would quickly find a common language. But isn't a nuclear disaster a more tangible danger than a landing by extraterrestrials? Isn't the ecological threat big enough? Don't all countries have a common stake in finding a sensible and fair approach to the problems of the developing states and peoples?[24]

Gorbachev went on to state that "the dialectics" of the current situation point to a "combination of competition and confrontation between" capitalism and communism within the context of a "growing independence of the countries of the world."[25] This was a startling statement in a country that had been founded on class struggle and unrelenting opposition to capitalist imperialism.

At the end of this section of his speech, Gorbachev appeared to move from relying on the old concept of "peaceful coexistence" to inviting the capitalist countries to "compete with us under the conditions of a durable peace" in an effort to create "worthy, truly human material and spiritual conditions of life for all nations, ensuring that our planet should be habitable, and in cultivating a caring attitude toward its riches, especially to man himself—the greatest treasure, and all his potentials."[26]

In his memoirs written in 1996, Robert Gates, Soviet specialist, senior CIA official under Reagan, and later head of the agency, wrote that Gorbachev's speech and the agenda he laid out at the Twenty-Seventh Congress "should be marked as the beginning of the end of the Cold War."[27]

Although Secretary of State Shultz did not fully realize the impact the Twenty-Seventh Congress was to have in the future, he did understand that Gorbachev's ideas were "new and bold," and that Soviet diplomacy was changing in a positive way. However, Weinberger and the CIA director William Casey had long ago decided the Soviet Union was an implacable enemy of the West and any soothing verbiage from them was nothing more than an attempt at distraction from their real goals.[28]

His memoirs notwithstanding, Robert Gates sided with Weinberger and Casey. In his presentations to Shultz and other senior officials, he misrepresented the conclusions of lower-level CIA analysts. In the late 1970s and 1980s, the analysts had believed the Soviet Union was undertaking a massive military buildup. But in early 1986, they concluded that they had been wrong and Soviet spending on strategic nuclear weapons had in fact declined by 40 percent. Most telling, the analysts concluded the Soviets had cut back their strategic weapons expenditures once they had reached strategic parity with the United States.

This was not what Weinberger, Casey, and Gates wanted to hear. According to former CIA analysts, Weinberger "went nuts." Weinberger and Gates were not about to endorse reports that the Soviets were pulling back from an arms race. And so they suppressed them. In a memo to Shultz, Gates characterized Gorbachev's January proposal as "tactically a clever stroke, [but it] did not change any basic Soviet position" on arms control. As FitzGerald notes, "As for Gorbachev's report to the Twenty-seventh Congress, Gates does not even pretend to have paid it any attention at the time."[29]

Despite the hostility from some members of his cabinet toward arms control and Gorbachev's evident frustration with the Reagan administration's response to his proposals, Reagan agreed to an offer from Gorbachev for an arms control summit in Reykjavík, Iceland, in October 1986.

Strobe Talbot, an academic and former State Department official under Bill Clinton, described the summit at Reykjavik as "one of the strangest episodes in the annals of nuclear diplomacy."[30] Reagan and Gorbachev almost upended decades of arms control agreements negotiated under the assumption of mutual assured destruction and replaced them all with a beautiful vision in which nuclear weapons would be eliminated entirely. Yet in the end, the vision disappeared as if a genie had jumped back into its bottle without fulfilling their wish, and the nightmare that had unfolded in the wake of Hiroshima remained as real as it ever was.

Upon Reagan's return to the capitol, Washington was in a major uproar. In the days and weeks following the summit, Reagan and members of his administration projected a bright sense of optimism. White House officials declared the talks had been a "breakthrough event." Progress toward arms control had been "momentous" and "historic," they claimed, despite the fact that the SDI remained an obstacle to concluding an agreement. In what White House Press Secretary Larry Speakes called "the super-blitz of all [news] blitzes," administration officials held about ninety press conferences in a single week; they even sent a "truth squad" to London, Paris, Rome, and Bonn.[31]

But people in Washington began requesting greater clarity as to just what Reagan and Gorbachev had discussed. The reports by American officials were inconsistent, and the fact that Gorbachev's account of the negotiations, given in a speech on October 14, was at odds with all of the American versions was disquieting to many.[32]

A few days later, a series of contradictory statements by administration officials led to controversy around whether Reagan had agreed to an end to all nuclear weapons, including bombers, or just nuclear missiles. The White House asserted it was just nuclear missiles.[33] On October 22, Gorbachev accused the United States of misrepresenting the negotiations. Two days later, a Soviet official read from their version of the minutes that stated the agreement was to include "the elimination of all strategic weapons" and that "all nuclear arms are to be eliminated."[34]

But even the prospect of eliminating just missiles was enough to horrify defense analysts. If ballistic missiles were eliminated, the only remaining nuclear forces would be bombers, and the Soviet Union had superior air defenses that would be very expensive for the United States to emulate.

NATO Allies were also incensed because under such an agreement they would have to give up their own missiles. British Prime Minister Margaret Thatcher complained, "It was like an earthquake. There was no place you could put your political feet, where you were certain that you could stand."[35]

James Schlesinger, the former Secretary of Defense under Richard Nixon and Gerald Ford, brought back the specter of the giant Red Army, a concern that would apply if strategic bombers were also eliminated:

For a generation, the security of the Western world has rested on nuclear deterrence. Its goal has been to deter not only nuclear attack but also massive conventional assault from the East. The American position at Reykjavik seems to have reflected no understanding of these simple fundamentals.[36]

Yet back in April, the Reagan administration had dismissed a proposal by Gorbachev for "a substantial reduction" of conventional forces in Europe. This reduction would be verified by on-site inspections and would cover the whole area "from the Atlantic Ocean to the Urals."[37] The distance from the Ural Mountains to the former Soviet Union's border with Europe is about one thousand miles.

The picture of the negotiations that eventually emerged was, as Larry Speakes explained, that the Americans viewed Reykjavík as "just another opportunity for Reagan and Gorbachev to meet in person; we embarked on the trip to Iceland without any great expectation of actually concluding an arms control agreement."[38]

Therefore, the United States was unprepared for serious negotiations. When the Soviets made their dramatic offers, the Americans soon realized they needed to respond in kind if they were to avoid giving the Soviets a propaganda victory. So they began improvising, offering more sweeping agreements, expecting the Soviets to reject them. To their surprise the Soviets responded with even more sweeping counterproposals.

Reagan carried matters to the next step with an offer to eliminate nuclear weapons entirely, something he had been advocating for years. When Gorbachev agreed to that, "there was nowhere else for Reagan to go," FitzGerald explains, "but back to the old issue of SDI . . . an argument he had down pat after dozens of repetitions. Reagan was furious when he walked out, and small wonder. Gorbachev had forced him to say *nyet*."[39]

Shultz and his negotiators were "crushed" because "Gorbachev had offered them the grand Compromise [they] had been working for two years to achieve, and they were incapable of making the deal. Adelman, on the other hand, was "not a bit depressed" because as he wrote: "Sure, the American people like their president to sit down with the Russians, but they like it even more when he stands up to the Russians." Gorbachev was angry that Reagan would not budge from his nonsensical notion of a strategic defense against nuclear missiles.[40]

As it turned out, months before the meeting at Reykjavík, the absurdity of the SDI was becoming apparent to political figures in both Washington and Moscow. Back in the summer of 1985, the Senate Appropriations Subcommittee on Defense had its staff members visit major SDI research laboratories around the country and interview the scientists working there. Their report, which was made public, contradicted the assurances from Weinberger, Abrahamson, and others that "genuine breakthroughs" had been achieved.[41]

In fact, the Senate study reported that the limited technical progress that had been achieved was outweighed by technical failures that illustrated how difficult it would be to create a space-based missile defense system. As some of the technical managers put it, the SDI systems were "too Buck Rodgers" and "too much in the 'if' stage" for them to become a reality in the foreseeable future.[42]

Some of the technical failures were the stuff of scandal, including a hundred-million-dollar appropriation for an X-ray laser project based on a test that had been a total failure. Yet the tests continued, even though no one saw them as having any use for strategic defense.[43] As FitzGerald points out, "In the view of the numerous SDI scientists . . . much of the progress that had been made in the program . . . lay in a greater understanding of the difficulties involved in mounting an effective strategic defense."[44]

Even the promise of the most promising technology was still "merely theoretical."[45] On top of all that, the Senate report came to the same conclusion the Soviets had: it would be far easier to attack or overwhelm a space-based missile defense than it would be to keep it operational.

In addition to a litany of other technical barriers, there was also the expense. The developments were on track to be "the largest military-research program the U.S. had ever undertaken. The total research costs would be in excess of the full deployment costs of many major weapons systems." Knowledgeable outsiders estimated the total cost of deployment at a trillion dollars. The directors of SDI development insisted that number was much too high, but they refused to offer an estimate of their own.[46]

Nonetheless, neither the technological nor the fiscal reality seemed to affect the political reality, at least where some politicians were concerned. In this instance, it was not Reagan but some members of Congress who insisted on staying in their "dream." When the budget bill for the following year allocated substantially less money for the SDI than had been requested, eight Republican members of Congress, including senators Malcolm Wallop, Dan Quayle, and Pete Wilson and Representatives Jack Kemp and Jim Courter, wrote a letter to Reagan:

> Mr. President, if the administration keeps on defining SDI as a faraway dream for the next millennium, no one will support it, including us. But if we begin now, as we must, to build the antimissile device we can build, the American people would soon enjoy real and growing protection.[47]

But even Reagan seemed to have a better grip on reality than some of his avid supporters. He wrote to Gorbachev proposing to delay the deployment of the SDI for seven and a half years. A few days later, he met with Senator Wallop and the others. He told them that "to deploy systems of limited effectiveness now would divert limited funds and delay our main research. It could well erode support for the program before it's permitted to reach its potential."[48]

In December 1987, Reagan reversed course once again when Weinberger, General Abrahamson, and Richard Perle delivered a glowing account of the state of research on the SDI, complete with charts and graphs. A White House official published an article claiming that by 1995 the U.S. could have an operational system that could disrupt a Soviet first strike. To congressional critics of the SDI, that sounded like a political move rather one based on technical reality. And indeed, one White House official supported a first-stage deployment of SDI quickly "so it will be in place and not tampered with by future administrations."[49] A senior scientist working on the SDI was even more blunt: "Like it or not, we see a political reality staring us in the face. If we don't come up with something specific, people are not going to let us play in the sand-box for ten years."[50]

In January of 1987 the conflict over the SDI in Washington started up again with renewed intensity when Weinberger publicly called for early deployment. Once more, officials in charge of technical development could provide little assurance that even a limited deployment would work. But it was neither politicians nor technicians who eventually forced the demise of the Strategic Defense Initiative. Instead, it was a most unlikely candidate: the chairman of the Pentagon's Joint Chiefs of Staff, Admiral William Crowe.

Crowe was disturbed by the way Weinberger and Abrahamson had been blatantly misrepresenting the viability of the SDI to Reagan. When, on one occasion, he heard the Secretary of Defense declare, "Mr. President, your dream is here," Crowe wrote, "I thought I was going to choke."[51] Crowe did publicly dispute the assertions of SDI advocates, including his boss, Secretary of Defense Weinberger. But his most effective move was a quiet bureaucratic maneuver: He convinced Weinberger and Abrahamson to have a limited or "phase one" version that SDI advocates were pressing for be brought into the formal Pentagon process for weapons acquisitions.[52]

Abrahamson agreed to Crowe's suggestion, thinking this would give the scheme more legitimacy in the Pentagon and Congress.

But he may not have realized just how rigorous the Pentagon's acquisition process was. The Defense Science Board in charge of the Pentagon evaluations established a minimum level of effectiveness the new system must meet, just as it would have for any for any other proposed system. In this case, the requirement was that it would stop 30 percent of missiles from a limited "'first-wave' attack."[53]

After the Defense Science Board found the initial plans for SDI phase one development too sketchy for it to draw any conclusions about its cost or effectiveness, political pressure kept the project alive longer than it might have survived on its own. But in the end the project simply faded away. Admiral Crowe later wrote that using the Pentagon's formal process "may have been the chiefs' most significant accomplishment on SDI."[54]

FitzGerald remarked that the Joint Chiefs had succeeded in turning the SDI back into a "research project" and had altered the political reality such that there was no way to "reinvest it with Reagan's magic"; "by luring Abrahamson into making a definite proposal, Admiral Crowe had performed the reverse alchemy of turning gold into dross—or magic into a weapons system that would cost billions upon billions of dollars and still let 70 percent of Soviet missiles through."[55]

Yet the SDI continued its dreamlike existence for a bit longer. On December 7, 1987, Gorbachev arrived in Washington for a summit meeting with Reagan. By that time, he was a celebrity to the American public. On that first night he dined with Henry Kissinger, Reverend Billy Graham, John Denver, and Yoko Ono. People lined the streets to see the man who was transforming the Soviet Union.[56]

The summit meeting, however, accomplished very little. As usual, Gorbachev came prepared with detailed proposals; Reagan was barely able to follow any of them and responded with feeble jokes. For the second day Reagan's staff had prepared a stack of notes, which he pulled out of a drawer after Gorbachev arrived at the Oval Office.[57] One of the items was a proposal that the Soviets agree to

U.S. deployment of the SDI at some future date, something that had never been suggested before. This new proposal was apparently included because a new secretary of defense, Frank Carlucci, had replaced Weinberger, and Carlucci needed some political cover with conservative proponents of Star Wars.[58]

Following his script, Reagan told Gorbachev, "We are going forward with the research and development necessary to see if this is a workable concept and if it is, we are going to deploy it."

Gorbachev, who hadn't even mentioned SDI at that point, replied calmly:

> Mr. President, you do what you think you have to do. . . . And if in the end you think you have a system you want to deploy, go ahead and deploy it. Who am I to tell you what to do? I think you're wasting money. I don't think it will work. But if that's what you want to do, go ahead. . . . We're moving in another direction, and we preserve our option to do what we think is necessary in our own national interest at the time. And we think we can do it less expensively and with greater effectiveness.[59]

Reagan managed to portray the summit to the public as a "clear success" that had greatly advanced the cause of arms control. His claim was hardly accurate, but it was a public relations success. It led to a substantial increase in his approval rating to 61 percent compared to 49 percent two months earlier. However, by the time Gorbachev left the U.S., his approval rating with the American public was at 65 percent.[60]

In May 1988, Reagan went to Moscow for one last summit meeting with Gorbachev. Again, very little was accomplished in terms of arms control or any other issues of concern between the United States and the Soviet Union. As a reporter for the *Washington Post* put it, the accords reached in Moscow "could have been accomplished by a couple of assistant secretaries of state in Geneva before lunch."[61]

But the summit was a resounding public relations success for Reagan and Gorbachev. This time it was Gorbachev who needed the favorable publicity. He was in the midst of promulgating his plan for *perestroika*, an extensive refashioning of Soviet society along more democratic lines. The changes formally separated the Communist Party from direct control over social functions, including the economy. Instead, there were to be elections for a national legislature, judicial independence, and individual rights for citizens.

A public show of newfound amity between the United States and the Soviet Union would go a long way toward reassuring Soviet citizens that the threat of the United States was fading, thus weakening the opposition of the political old guard. In one remarkable scene, Gorbachev guided Reagan through Red Square, followed by television cameras. They chatted with each other and small groups of people who had been allowed into the square. Gorbachev even picked up a small boy and invited him to "shake hands with Grandfather Reagan." The two leaders cuddled the child as if campaigning for election together.

Back inside the Kremlin grounds, a reporter asked the president what had become of the "evil empire" he had warned about in 1983. "I was talking about another time, another era," the President replied.[62] It was mission accomplished for Gorbachev: *perestroika* moved forward, setting off a series of events that led to the breakup of the Soviet Union in 1991.

There have been numerous claims that it was the financial stress caused by the necessity of countering Star Wars that pushed the Soviet Union into dissolution. However, historians Frances FitzGerald and Pavel Podvig agree that there is little evidence to support those claims. Soviet spending on strategic weapons did not increase significantly during that time, nor did overall military spending, despite the fact that they were fighting a war in

Afghanistan. Podvig points out that according to Soviet estimates, "technical counter-measures to defeat missile defenses would have cost no more than five percent of their SDI-like program."[63]

The end of the Soviet Union did not end the sense of military peril political conservatives in the U.S. felt themselves and sought to engender in others. Gorbachev seemed to understand this aspect of America's political culture very well. In April 1988, Shultz and Colin Powell—the national security advisor at the time—met with Gorbachev in preparation for the upcoming summit meeting. Gorbachev talked to them about his plans for changing Soviet society. Then, with a playful look, he asked: "What are you going to do now that you've lost your best enemy?"[64]

CHAPTER 15

The Indispensable Nation

The Soviet Union officially dissolved on December 26, 1991, when its governing body, the Supreme Soviet, voted the U.S.S.R. out of existence and recognized the newly established Commonwealth of Independent States in its place. By that time, the United States had already found its new enemy. On January 16, 1991, President George H. W. Bush announced a military assault against Iraq, specifically against its dictator, Saddam Hussein.

The first Gulf War was the U.S. response to Iraq's invasion of the neighboring oil kingdom of Kuwait. The war's objective was to expel Iraqi troops from Kuwait and protect the oil fields of neighboring Saudi Arabia. Desert Storm appeared to be a stunning success that demonstrated America's overwhelming military superiority over Iraqi forces. Acting in conjunction with a coalition of military forces from several countries, including Britain and France, the United States used conventional air and ground forces to quickly overwhelm Iraq's army.

At the conflict's conclusion, many people—especially those outside the United States and Western Europe—believed that most countries in the world were potential enemies of the United States. Iraq did not pose a military threat to the United States, nor was it closely aligned with a nation that did pose such a threat as the Soviet Union once had. What Iraq had done was threaten America's control over Middle Eastern oil. It was only logical that people in other parts of the world would wonder what natural resources they had that the United States might someday consider vital to its interests. What domestic or international policies might their country adopt that the United States might consider threatening to its global hegemony?

In 1998, then American UN ambassador and later secretary of state Madeleine Albright clarified the matter in an interview in which she claimed the United States was the "indispensable nation"[1] and told the UN the United States would "behave multi-laterally when we can and unilaterally when we must" to protect its "national interests."[2]

America's self-proclaimed status as the indispensable nation helped ensure there would be no meaningful progress in lessening the danger of nuclear war. In fact, the United States' belief that it had the right to control other nations set it on a path toward end-less conventional wars as it sought to enforce its hegemony over the world economy in general and strengthen its control over the world's oil supply in particular.

But this view of America as the dominant world power did not begin with the disintegration of the Soviet Union. American leaders in 1945 already knew that the old European powers, their cities in ruins after World War II, would barely be able to help themselves let alone maintain their colonial empires. With the atomic bomb in its pocket, America had been poised to dominate the world like no nation had ever done before, but the Soviet Union had stood in the way. Now, with its rival in disarray, America's political and business leaders were ready to take what they believed was their true place in the world.

Although nuclear weapons served as a menacing context for America's claim to worldwide hegemony, the immediate threat to any country that dared to defy the United States was a con-ventional military one. Russia's leaders were not reassured by the United States' ability to use conventional forces to impose its will in

Iraq. They saw this ability as a potential threat to their border with Western Europe. The Russians realized their conventional forces were relatively weak and could not stand up to the military strength of U.S. and its NATO allies.

Iraq had a development program for nuclear weapons in the 1970s and 80s that it later abandoned. As Lawrence Freedman, a leading academic authority on nuclear strategy, suggested, it was reasonable for the Russians to ask, "Would the United States . . . have been so ready to go to war on Kuwait's behalf in 1991 if Iraq's nuclear program had reached maturity—even assuming that the Kuwaitis and Saudis themselves would not have capitulated already to Iraqi demands?"[3]

The logical conclusion for Russian leaders, Freedman suggests, was "that they had to forget past promises never to use nuclear weapons first and revive deterrence as their best option" against the powerful military forces stationed along their western border by the United States and an ascendant NATO. In effect, the postwar logic the United States used to justify its use of nuclear deterrence— that it was the best way to prevent the powerful Red Army from overwhelming Europe—was now reversed: The Russians believed they needed nuclear weapons to deter the threat of a conventional military attack by the United States and its Allies.

America's behavior toward Iraq after the war was equally alarming. Since the goal of the war had been only to expel Iraq's troops from Kuwait, Bush did not send the U.S. military to Baghdad to overthrow Hussein himself. Instead, in 1991, the Bush administration prompted the United Nations to institute broad economic sanctions against the Hussein government, banning the importation of anything that could be used to create weapons of mass destruction, e.g., nuclear, chemical, or biological weapons. The United States was to enforce the ban.

The Clinton administration also bombed Iraq on several occasions during the 1990s. There was a cruise missile attack on

Baghdad in 1993, then a larger-scale attack in December 1998 called Operation Desert Fox. On October 31 of that year, Clinton signed the Iraq Liberation Act, which appropriated funds to support opposition groups within Iraq dedicated to overthrowing Saddam Hussein. In other words, the American goal of "regime change" in Iraq was in place well before President George Bush's 2003 invasion of the country, officially called Operation Iraqi Freedom.

At the time of the 9/11 attack against the World Trade Center in New York in 2001, the United States had already invaded Afghanistan in order to dislodge the Taliban government there and was trying to capture Osama bin Laden, the al-Qaeda leader who had organized the World Trade Center attack. To some observers, it seemed odd that the United States would suddenly pivot from that battle to focus on Iraq which had no connection to the attack.

The shift may have seemed like an odd choice from a purely military perspective, but it made sense in political terms. Saddam Hussein's regime was an easy target for an American military built to overwhelm an opponent in a traditional military conflict. On the other hand, the U.S. had no clear understanding of what it meant to destroy a shadowy, nebulous network like al-Qaeda.

The 2001 Authorization to Use Military Force passed by Congress gave Bush the authority to launch military operations against "those nations, organizations, or persons he determines" were involved in the World Trade Center attack. By making that determination concerning Iraq, Bush was able to give America the satisfaction of destroying an enemy of long standing and also offer the American public what looked like an early victory in the newly declared Global War Against Terror.

The fact that Iraq had nothing to do with the attack on the World Trade Center and was never a serious threat to the security of the United States was of no relevance in political terms. Americans could believe the country had reclaimed a sense of potency after what felt like a debilitating assault against Fortress America. Many

Americans wanted to see their country as the powerful bastion of righteousness Reagan described in his Star Wars speech back in 1983: "The defense policy of the United States is based on a simple premise: The United States does not start fights. We will never be an aggressor. We maintain our strength in order to deter and defend against aggression—to preserve freedom and peace."[4]

Yet the manner in which the United States enforced the 1990 sanctions against Iraq over the previous decade led many people at home and abroad to indeed view America as a merciless aggressor. The ban included "dual use" items that could be used for both military and civilian purposes. That category included such items as chlorine, which could be used to make poison gas but was also needed for water purification plants. Limits were also placed on the importation of medical supplies and pharmaceuticals.[5]

According to a 1995 UN-sponsored report, these sanctions led to the preventable deaths of over 500,000 Iraqi children. In a 1996 interview on CBS's *60 Minutes*, host Lesley Stahl asked Madeleine Albright, American Ambassador to the UN, "We have heard that a half million children have died. I mean, that's more children than died in Hiroshima. And, you know, is the price worth it?" Albright replied, "I think this is a very hard choice, but the price—we think the price is worth it."[6]

As Ambassador Hasmy Agam of Malaysia put it at the UN Security Council in 2000: "How ironic is it that the same policy that is supposed to disarm Iraq of its weapons of mass destruction has itself become a weapon of mass destruction."[7]

Also very disturbing to anyone who was paying close attention were some of the other statements Albright made in the interview in which she declared the United States to be the indispensable nation.

> It is the threat of the use of force . . . that is going to put force behind the diplomacy. But if we have to use force, it is because we are America; we are the indispensable nation. We

stand tall and we see further than other countries into the future, and we see the danger here to all of us. I know that the American men and women in uniform are always prepared to sacrifice for freedom, democracy, and the American way of life.[8]

Albright's claim that America is the "indispensable nation" was much more than the opinion of a single government official; it was already American policy in both principle and deed. The policy applied to virtually every part of the world, not just the Middle East.

Andrew Bacevich, former army colonel and professor emeritus of international relations and history at Boston University, pointed out in his book *The New American Militarism* that only six large-scale overseas U.S. military operations took place during the Cold War from 1945 through 1988. There were nine such operations from 1989 through 2003, starting with the overthrow of Nicaragua's Manuel Noriega in 1989 and ending with the Iraq War in 2003. "And that count does not include . . . Bill Clinton's signature cruise missile attacks against obscure targets in obscure places, the almost daily bombing of Iraq throughout the late 1990s, or the quasi-combat missions that have seen GIs dispatched to Rwanda, Colombia, East Timor, and the Philippines."[9]

The new American militarism Bacevich describes is indeed new. The United States has always been an expansionist power. The "winning of the West" at the expense of Native Americans; the Mexican–American War; the colonization of Puerto Rico; dominance in the Philippines; and military interventions in much of Latin America attest to that. However, from the time of America's founding until the end of World War II, the United States took James Madison's warning seriously: "The means of defense against foreign danger have been always the instruments of tyranny at home," and thus a "standing military force, with an overgrown Executive will not long be safe companions to liberty."[10]

The United States did raise large military forces when facing a major war, but it radically reduced the number of soldiers once the military crisis was over. Bacevich notes that at the end of World War II there were over eight million officers and enlisted men and women in the U.S. Army. Two years later that number had been reduced by 75 percent, and the army's "combat capabilities [were] virtually nonexistent."[11] A similar process had ensued at the end of the Civil War and World War I.

But World War II was different. When it ended, the United States alone had the atomic bomb. America's atomic monopoly, it was assumed, would enable America to lay down the rules for international order as well as to act as the world's "policeman."

CHAPTER 16

A More Reasonable
Form of Violence

nce the Soviet Union developed its own nuclear weapons in the late 1940s, the United States could no longer think in terms of dictating the international order. But in terms of ongoing geopolitics, the Soviet threat to the nations near its borders was primarily a conventional military one. As far as the world's economy was concerned, that threat was barely a factor at all. Throughout the Cold War, the United States' strategy for dealing with the Soviet Union was to contain its military while expanding America's worldwide economic power and political influence. Doing so meant using conventional warfare in a manner that would extend American authority without posing a direct threat to the vital interests of the Soviet Union.

Within this context, Andrew Bacevich describes a new cohort of strategic theorists who thrived during that time in such institutions as Harvard, MIT, the University of Chicago, and Daniel Ellsberg's old employer, the RAND Corporation. One of their concerns, as Herman Kahn, a prominent strategist at RAND, suggested, was finding "more reasonable forms of using violence."[1] In other words, reviving the venerable notion of war as "politics by other means" through the use of conventional warfare in a nuclear world. These theorists developed the concept of a "limited war," one in which "the aim was not to crush the enemy but to bring him to the realization that ending the war on your terms served *his own* [italics in the original] interests."[2] This approach to conventional warfare during the Cold War eventually formed the basis for America's declaring itself the all-powerful "indispensable nation" once the Cold War was over.

One of the most prominent advocates of this idea was another RAND employee, Albert Wohlstetter. Wohlstetter theorized that "the greater economic resources of the West offer many advantages in a war of attrition" because economically weaker opponents would be unable to sustain such a war and forced to seek a compromise that would work to America's advantage. By the early 1960s, Secretary of Defense McNamara saw Wohlstetter's concept of limited war as a way to counter the Communist insurgency in Vietnam.[3]

Unfortunately for American aspirations, the North Vietnamese and their Viet Cong allies in South Vietnam saw the American presence in the country as an existential threat rather than the occasion for the cost–benefit analysis Wohlstetter had theorized. If they understood the carefully calculated applications of American force as signals to bargain for a mutually acceptable outcome, they had no interest in such bargaining. They certainly were not willing to accept the "compromise" Washington had in mind: the establishment of South Vietnam as a nation separate from North. They were willing to fight to the death—and the United States was not. America's economic power was greater, but the Vietnamese's will to fight was greater still. The result was a disaster for the United States.[4]

American leaders, least of all Wohlstetter, were not ready to give up on the idea of using military force to extend and secure America's power throughout the world. The computer chip, Wohlstetter believed, was the key to dominance. By 1974, he was advocating an "expanding family of precision guided munitions" that allowed for "much more effective and discriminating application of force in an increasingly wider variety of political and operational circumstanc-es."[5] These weapons were supposedly so precise they could strike only military targets and leave bystanders unharmed.

The idea was that the United States would not merely respond to acts of military aggression by others. Instead, according to an influential 1988 government report, the United States could "bring force to bear effectively, with discrimination and in time to thwart any of a wide range of plausible aggressions."[6] In other words, American politicians could bomb whomever they thought needed to be bombed. As Bacevich commented,

> Here was the final piece in the evolving logic that pointed to-ward a strategy of preventive war: by their very existence dic-tatorships constituted an unacceptable threat. The only sure remedy to the problem of vulnerability—the true . . . strategy of deterrence in a nuclear age—was to bring despotic regimes into full compliance with American norms, using force if necessary to do so. . . . For his part, Wohlstetter believed that precise and discriminating U.S. military capabilities now made a policy of regime change feasible, if only responsible political authorities had the wit and the gumption to act."[7]

By the time Wohlstetter died in 1997, his cause had already been taken up by a senior analyst at the Department of Defense, Andrew Marshall. Marshall expanded on Wohlstetter's concepts concern-ing information technology and warfare with what he called the Revolution in Military Affairs (RMA).

> By the mid-1990s, [the RMA] had established itself among specialists as the authoritative frame of reference with-in which the debate over the future of warfare unfolded. Although few remarked upon the fact, the earlier revolu-tion of 1945—the one that had supposedly made war itself

obsolete—now shrank to seeming insignificance. The RMA promised war a brand-new lease on life.[8]

Marshall predicted that "long-range precision strike weapons coupled to systems of sensors and to command and control systems will . . . come to dominate much of warfare" and thus, as Bacevich explained, "make it possible to hit and kill anything anywhere on the planet at any time" through the use of superior computer technology. These capabilities, Marshall claimed, would make the United States the world's permanent dominant military power. In essence, Marshall was reviving General Leslie Groves's vision of a worldwide American military empire. Only this time, Marshall believed American dominance would be achieved not with the atomic bomb but rather with the computer. "Obtaining early superiority in the information realm," he claimed, "will become central to success in future warfare."[9]

This globalized view of warfare soon became linked to economic globalization. In 1999 the *New York Times* columnist Thomas Friedman wrote that

> sustainable globalization still requires a stable, geopolitical power structure, which simply cannot be maintained without the active involvement of the United States. . . . The hidden hand of the market will never work without a hidden fist— McDonald's cannot flourish without McDonnell Douglas, the builder of the F-15. And the hidden fist that keeps the world safe for Silicon Valley's technologies is called the United States Army, Air Force, Navy and Marine Corps.[10]

Robert Kagan, a historian and former member of the Council on Foreign Relations, agreed that America's military needed a free hand to ensure the freedom of the marketplace: "Good ideas and technologies need a strong power that promotes those ideas by example and protects those ideas by winning on the battlefield."[11]

But why were these wars being fought in the Middle East? Was Saddam Hussein refusing to allow his people to buy our hamburgers and computer chips? Other explanations were equally suspect. If replacing oppressive governments with ones based on the principles of American democracy was necessary for United States' security, Saudi Arabia would have been another conspicuous target. The most obvious answer is also probably the most accurate: the United States needed to control the region to ensure it had access to oil.

America's path to fighting wars in the Middle East began during the Carter administration when America's long-standing relationship with oil-producing states in the Middle East began to unravel. But the stage had been set a few years earlier.[12]

U.S. oil production peaked in the early 1970s. Facing a shortage of oil, the Nixon administration authorized the importation of more oil from the Middle East. However, in October of 1973, the Yom Kippur War broke out between Israel on one side and Syria and Egypt on the other. The Organization of the Petroleum Exporting Countries (OPEC), a consortium of oil-producing countries from around the world, placed an embargo against the United States in response to its support of Israel. At the time, the bulk of OPEC's members were in the Middle East, including Saudi Arabia, Iraq, and other Persian Gulf states.

Soon after, gasoline shortages led to long lines and high prices at American gas stations across the country. The United States and OPEC reached an accommodation in 1974, but low gasoline prices were gone, never to return.[13]

When Jimmy Carter took office in 1977, one of the first things he did was to push for energy independence. In 1979 he delivered what is remembered as his Crisis of Confidence speech in which he told Americans they needed to live more frugally in order to preserve America's ability to control its own destiny.[14] He called for Americans to use public transportation more often and set their thermostats a bit lower. "Energy," Carter declared, "will be the immediate test of our ability to unite this Nation, and it can also be the standard around which we rally. On the battlefield of energy we can win for our Nation a new confidence, and we can seize control again of our common destiny."[15]

Carter also emphasized the need for alternative sources of energy that could be developed domestically. To be sure, his plan was not intended to address climate change, an issue that was barely on the edge of public awareness at the time. Carter simply called for using more coal and other fossil fuels that were abundant within the United States. But he did set "the crucial goal of 20 percent of our energy coming from solar power by the year 2000."[16]

However, the American people were not ready to accept Carter's assertion that limiting their use of fossil fuels was the path to "more freedom, more confidence . . . [and] much more control over our own lives." For them, abundance was a defining feature of the American way of life.

Reagan was quick to make use of this political opening in 1979 when he announced his entry into the 1980 presidential campaign. "First we must decide that 'less' is not enough. . . . It is no program simply to say 'use less energy.'"[17]

In his State of the Union speech in January 1980, Carter reversed his position on frugality and moved on to securing access to Middle East oil, by force if necessary. In doing so, he was responding to a fundamental change in the geopolitics of the Middle East. For over three decades, the United States had been able to use its political and economic power to dominate the region.

In 1945, Franklin D. Roosevelt had met with King Ibn Saud of Saudi Arabia on an American warship anchored in the Suez Canal. King Saud agreed to grant the United States privileged access to Saudi oil in exchange for American security guarantees.[18] The United States chose to use its influence behind the scenes by relying on surrogates to implement those security agreements. For the first few years, the British played that role. Later, the U.S. relied on the Shah of Iran. The U.S. also hired corporate military contractors for training and other military support to its client states in the region.

All that changed in 1979 with the Iranian Revolution. Suddenly, Iran was controlled by a regime that was hostile to the United States. To make matters worse, the Soviet Union invaded Afghanistan, potentially threatening American military supremacy in the Persian Gulf.[19]

In his State of the Union speech, Carter enunciated what has become known as the Carter Doctrine: "An attempt by any outside force to gain control of the Persian Gulf region will be regarded as an assault on the vital interests of the United States of America, and such an assault will be repelled by any means necessary, including military force."[20]

A policy of self-reliance and commonsense frugality, one that would appear to be in keeping with America's most cherished national values, was to be replaced by one of military aggression in order to maintain unfettered material consumption as the basis of American freedom. The Carter Doctrine continues to this day as the bedrock of American Middle East policy.

Over the last decade, new drilling techniques have allowed American oil companies to tap into domestic supplies of gas and oil that were formerly inaccessible. As a result, America is once again a net exporter of fossil fuels. Nonetheless, the United States appears determined to continue enforcing the Carter Doctrine. The global economy is built on oil. Its factories need oil; industrial agricultural uses fossil-based fertilizers; plastics are derived from oil; the ships and planes that move the goods of the global economy around the globe run on oil. When it comes to making sure oil is readily available for the global market, the hidden hand is paired with a very visible fist.

The Revolution in Military Affairs has not supplanted its

pre-revolutionary nuclear counterpart. However, Marshall's "long-range precision strike weapon" has come to play a significant role in the global war to make the world safe for oil in the form of the armed drone. The drone operator can launch a missile against his target in Pakistan, Afghanistan, or Yemen while safely ensconced in an office in Virginia or Nevada.

The language American officials use to justify drone attacks is very much like that used by the advocates of the RMA, only in some cases with a particularly virulent and dehumanizing slant. For example, in 2012, John Brennan, then assistant to the president for homeland security and counterterrorism in the Barack Obama administration, said, "It's this surgical precision, the ability, with laser-like focus, to eliminate the cancerous tumor called an al-Qaida terrorist while limiting damage to the tissue around it, that makes this counterterrorism tool so essential."

Seemingly oblivious to the irony, he goes on to quote from Obama's Nobel Peace Prize speech: "'I believe the United States of America must remain a standard bearer in the conduct of war. That is what makes us different from those whom we fight. That is a source of our strength.'"[21]

Some Americans may view terrorists as less than human. But in truth, their behavior, although unjustifiable, is not hard to understand. As one commentator put it,

> Terrorism is . . . the natural recourse of the weak and dispossessed of this world. . . . It is entirely understandable why comfortable and powerful states find terrorism reprehensible. . . . Although deliberately targeting civilians is a long step into barbarism, it is not so clear why bombs delivered by planes and rockets are less objectionable morally, at least to the victims of the "collateral damage," than bombs strapped onto the bodies of suicidal terrorists.[22]

One might add that if targeting civilians is a long step into bar-barism, the United States and Britain marched very far down that path with their "area bombing" during the Second World War. Then, of course, there is Hiroshima and Nagasaki.

Brennan and Obama may have thought that with drones, they had finally found some new "more reasonable forms of using vio-lence" to achieve military objectives as well as economic ones. More likely they were simply repeating a well-worn pattern. Eighty years ago "strategic bombing" was to be the surgical device that would make war less fatal to civilians. It quickly devolved into something quite different.

With drones, as with other "surgical strikes" over the years, the "tool" is much less precise than its advocates claim. In the case of drones, it turns out the definition of "combatant" includes all men of military age in the vicinity of the attack. The logic is eerily rem-iniscent of that behind the slide from precision bombing to area bombing in World War II. Who is considered a legitimate target ends up being determined by the capabilities of the weapon rather than the moral standards of those who employ it.[23]

The Military Industrial Complex

James Madison's warning about a large military coupled with an "overgrown Executive" should give us pause when we realize the United States military budget is now larger than that of the next seven biggest military spenders combined. The fact that 53 percent of all discretionary spending at the federal level is allocated to the military is alarming. So how did we get here? As it turns out, those soaring budgets and the administrative infrastructure to manage them began with the Manhattan Project.[1]

The Manhattan Project was "the largest and most expensive weapons research and development project ever undertaken up to that time," and it "absorbed a large proportion of the nation's scientific and engineering talent."[2] The project was also unusual for its time in that it brought in civilian scientists to work on military projects administered by military officers. Vannevar Bush took the initiative in this regard, having observed that "scientific trends [were] becoming a determining factor in warfare."[3]

As odd as it might seem today, not everyone in the military saw any reason to involve civilian scientists in military research. Early in the war, before he became involved with the Manhattan Project, Vannevar Bush suggested to navy officials that they might find civilian scientists helpful on a project involving anti-submarine warfare. However, he was told that it "needed no help along these lines." Bush found the army to be much more open to consultations with civilian scientists. It was his experience successfully integrating civilians into a military project that led Bush to put the Manhattan Project under the auspices of the army.[4]

The civilian scientists at the Manhattan Project, especially those from academia, chafed at the restrictions on their work put in place by the military. Robert Oppenheimer, the scientific director of the Manhattan Project, feared his laboratory team would be forced to take directions from their military superiors and would "thus in effect lose its scientific autonomy." He suggested that the laboratory be demilitarized, believing "the *solidarity of physicists* [italics in the original] is such that if these conditions are not met," they would have difficulty hiring more scientists, and "many of the men who have already planned to join the new Laboratory will reconsider commitments or come with such misgivings as to reduce their usefulness."[5]

Groves insisted on a traditional military security arrangement under which information was "compartmentalized" so that it could only be shared between scientists on a need-to-know basis. This arrangement was totally alien to scientists for whom the cross-fertilization of ideas and information was the very basis of successful research. They couldn't know in advance what they needed to know, and the key to a scientific breakthrough was often something they had never thought of before.

There were, of course, legitimate concerns about security leaks, and many scientists later acknowledged that Groves was an able administrator. But Groves felt open discussion by scientists was a waste of time. Better to force them "to mind their own jobs and not everyone else's." Groves applied a sports metaphor: "Just as outfielders should not think about the manager's job of changing the pitchers, and a blocker should not be worrying about the ball-carrier fumbling, each scientist had to be made to do his own work."[6]

One incident in this matter was particularly telling in other ways. When Groves learned the scientists were breaking his rules by holding weekly colloquiums, he agreed to Oppenheimer's request to allow the meetings to continue. However, Sherwin notes compartmentalization "had an additional, political dimension" in that it "also came to be used to restrict discussion of the implications of the development of atomic bombs." Groves allowed the meetings to continue provided the participants "avoid matters that, whatever their importance in other ways, were of little scientific interest."[7]

Shortly before the end of the war, Vannevar Bush laid out his proposals for government-directed scientific research for military purposes. In a report to President Truman, Bush declared, "There must be more—and more adequate—military research in peacetime. It is essential that the civilian scientists continue in peacetime some portion of those contributions to national security which they have made so effectively during the war."[8]

He expanded on the theme in a book published in 1946, *Endless Horizons*.

> Our present military and naval organizations were built for much more static armament than we have today. In the days of wooden ships and iron men it was not only sufficient, it was highly desirable, to place the full responsibility upon one officer to see to it that those ships were soundly built, and upon another to see that their guns were the best that could be constructed. We have come a long way from that situation, both in techniques and in organization; but our techniques have outrun our organization for handling them.[9]

Today "modern weapons call for complex programs involving many skills" and require the precise weaving together of technical capabilities, relying on the military's own resources coupled with "private laboratories for research tasks."[10]

Government support for military spending rose steadily during the 1950s. By 1956, almost four-fifths of the government's $3.45 billion research budget was allocated to the Department of Defense. The next year, the Soviet Union launched Sputnik, the world's first orbiting satellite. Fears that the Soviets would overtake the United States in science and technology led to a large increase in the federal government's funding of scientific research, both civilian and military.[11] Not surprisingly, the military took a disproportionate share. According to one study, by the 1980s, the United States was spending twice as much on military research and development as it did "on all other social goals put together."[12]

Whatever qualms about doing military research university scientists had during the war, they often had little choice a few decades later. Moreover, the Defense Department's funding extended well beyond what was once thought to be the boundaries of military research. A professor of public health facing funding cuts from the National Institutes of Health in 1983 applied for money from the Defense Department, lamenting, "I have forty people working for me. I can't wait until a disaster occurs to look for other sources of funding."[13] As Richard DeLauer, Undersecretary of Defense for Research and Engineering under President Reagan, put it, "The fact [is] that other elements of funding [have] slowed down. And it's surprising how many converts that makes."[14]

In his book *The New Politics of Science*, David Dickson makes a crucial point concerning the relationship of the universities, the government, and business corporations in the 1980s:

[T]he military has been able to reinforce the universities' own attempts to reject direct democratic control over the contents of their research programs (even if this means substitution of control by military authorities). It has . . . [allowed] university scientists to select their own research topics within fields considered broadly relevant to military needs. And it has actively encouraged private companies to tighten their links with the university research community, in particular by . . . offering bonuses to companies that subcontract some of their work to university scientists.[15]

This relationship, Dickson points out, "builds [the universities] into the structure of a weapons economy that they have an active interest in helping to maintain and expand."[16]

That relationship also helps create a politicized academia that has aligned itself with the ideological demands of corporations. In 1983, the American Council on Education presented a report to President Reagan, "America's Competitive Challenge." Prepared by a task force cochaired by the chairman and CEO of Rockwell International and the president of the University of California, the report declared its opposition to "national economic planning, income redistribution, and plant-closing restrictions."[17]

Defense spending was only about 30 percent of discretionary spending in 1983, compared to 53 percent in 2019. Today, the implications for such distorted budgetary priorities reach even farther than the corruption of educational institutions. The resulting deficits pose a threat to the survival of the United States in much the same way an outsized defense budget helped bring about the dissolution of the Soviet Union.

In 1976, a young French demographer named Emmanuel Todd published a book, *The Final Fall*, first in France and then in the United States in 1979. He used publicly available Soviet statistics. "Shabby and false" as they were, they still provided insights into the state of affairs within the Soviet Union. "Internal pressures are pushing the Soviet system to the breaking point," he wrote. "In ten, twenty, or thirty years, an astonished world will be witness to the dissolution or the collapse of this, the first of the Communist systems." According to historian and journalist Richard Rhodes, Todd pointed to the "'sluggishness' of the centralized Soviet economy" and "'lack of common sense on the part of Stalinist economists. . . .

How is it possible for a central organization to coordinate the activity of 250 million Soviet inhabitants, distributed over 22 million square kilometers, by arbitrarily fixing prices and wages?'"[18]

As Rhodes reports, Todd went on to explain how the "enormous portion of national revenue" devoted to the military served, "among other things, *to maintain the preeminence of the centralized sector of the economy* [italics in the original]." Meanwhile, Marxist ideas were turned "into an empty, meaningless litany," while "the official ideology" served to "transform Marx's texts into a collection of high-sounding but irrelevant rhetoric."[19]

At first glance, the situation in the Soviet Union was very different from that in the United States. However, the two countries were mirror images of each other in some very important respects. Where the economy of the Soviet Union was tightly cosseted, that of the United States appeared radically unfettered. Yet power and wealth in the United States was rapidly becoming ever more centralized. And as the growing confluence of universities, the government, and corporations illustrates, militarization was a driving force behind that trend.

As a result, the rhetoric of free markets providing opportunity for every American, no matter where on the social scale that person started from, rings increasingly hollow. Capitalism has transformed itself into socialism for the rich. In the Soviet Union, those who questioned the system were severely punished. In the United States, they were sometimes punished if their protests struck too close to the bone of the corporate body politic. But for the most part, they were simply ignored.

With regards to labor, Todd compared the U.S.S.R. of the 1970s to Europe in the 1860s:

In Communist countries the working class is frequently fired upon, as they were in Western Europe during the nineteenth century. They have personally witnessed what is a set piece of Marxist art and literature. . . . Communism has all the legendary vices of the capitalism condemned by Marx: misery, class conflict, and alienation.[20]

Todd's comments contain multiple ironies. During the first two decades after World War II, one could easily argue that the American working class had more influence over their country's economy and a larger share of its wealth than Soviet workers did over theirs. But by the time Todd was writing, the power and economic condition of American workers had begun a steep decline. In the Soviet Union, there was what the Russian people called the *nomenklatura*, a class of senior bureaucrats with access to better food, housing, medical care, and education than everyone else. The United States has a similar class of people. Americans sometimes refer to them as the "Establishment." The members of the American Establishment are typically found at the confluence of corporations, universities, and government.

One indication that the United States might be headed for a decline similar to that of the old Soviet Union is the state of America's infrastructure. Every four years the American Society of Civil Engineers' "Report Card for America's Infrastructure" assigns individual grades to each of sixteen categories such as airports, dams, bridges, drinking water, and hazardous waste. The report for 2021 gives the United States an overall grade of C–. The highest grades were a B for rail transportation and a B– for ports. Nothing else was above a C+. Dams, levees, roads, and stormwater received D grades.

The report lays out the consequences for American citizens: By 2039 the United States will have suffered $10 trillion in losses to its GDP, $2.4 trillion in exports, and three million jobs at a cost to the average American household of $3,300 a year.

Tellingly, the infrastructure report began in 1988 as a federally funded project, but the government stopped updating it after ten years. The ASCE began producing the report on its own in 1998 using the same methodology.[21]

CHAPTER 18

Cold War Redux

Our roads and bridges may be deteriorating and hazardous waste may be polluting our lakes and streams, but military spending continues at unsustainable levels. That spending also includes a major financial commitment to a modernization program that will make our nuclear weaponry more dangerous than ever.[1] Ironically, the increased spending and the increased danger stem from efforts by the Obama administration to reduce the likelihood of a nuclear conflict by reaching a new arms control agreement with Russia.

In his first year in office, President Obama vowed to work toward the elimination of nuclear weapons, a promise that contributed to his winning the Nobel Peace Prize in 2009. By the middle of 2010, his administration had negotiated the New Strategic Arms Treaty (New START) with Russia. The treaty calls for a substantial reduction in the total number of warheads allowed to each side. The official number is 1,550, but because of the somewhat arcane and counterintuitive method of counting, the actual number is closer to 2,000. Regardless, the reductions were substantial; the previous limit was 6,000.[2] However, because of Republican opposition in the Senate, Obama was forced to agree to the nuclear weapons modernization program to get the treaty passed.

According to a Congressional Budget Office (CBO) estimate, modernizing the United States' nuclear weapons will cost at least $1.25 trillion over thirty years, not counting the all-too-common

Pentagon cost overruns.[3]

Whatever strains the modernization program may place on America's future finances, it is part of the reason William Perry, the former secretary of defense under Bill Clinton, believes "the danger of a nuclear catastrophe today is greater than it was during the Cold War."[4] According to a 2017 special report from Reuters, "both sides are increasing exponentially the killing power of these weapons, upgrading the delivery vehicles so that they are bigger, more accurate and equipped with dangerous new features—without increasing the number of warheads or vehicles."[5]

For example, the air force has transformed the nuclear bomb it has long used on its bombers into a controllable "smart bomb" with a guidance system to ensure it detonates at precisely the intended target. Thus, the "smart" technology originally intended to enable "more reasonable forms of using violence" has been repurposed to make a bomb with twenty-three times the explosive power of the one dropped over Hiroshima even less "reasonable" than it had been before.

Worse still is a new "fuzing" device for the submarine-launched Trident II missiles. Previously, submarine-launched missiles were considerably less accurate than their land-based counterparts.

For this reason they were more suitable as a deterrent force that would respond to an enemy first-strike attack.[6]

But as the *Bulletin of the Atomic Scientists* points out,

this increase in capability is astonishing—boosting the overall killing power of existing US ballistic missile forces by a factor of roughly three—and it creates exactly what one would expect to see, if a nuclear-armed state were planning to have the capacity to fight and win a nuclear war by disarming enemies with a surprise first strike.[7]

As a result, there is more impetus on both sides to launch an attack based on evidence that a first strike may be imminent: "The new kill capability created by super-fuzing increases the tension and the risk that US or Russian nuclear forces will be used in response to early warning of an attack—even when an attack has not occurred."[8]

America's long history of threatening to use nuclear weapons adds an additional layer of risk to any nuclear crisis. Daniel Ellsberg lists twenty-five occasions where the United States threatened to use tactical nuclear weapons, starting with their actual use against Japan, followed by the implied threat during the Berlin Blockade in 1948, all the way to Bill Clinton's nuclear threat against Libya regarding an underground chemical weapons facility in 1996.[9]

Many of the threats were implicit but clear and public, as in Berlin in 1948. Others were explicit but secret, as were Nixon's threats of nuclear escalations against the North Vietnamese during the Vietnam War and the "'Diplomatic use of the Bomb' (Nixon's description) to deter Soviet unilateral action against the British and French in the Suez crisis of 1956."[10]

Some of the incidents Ellsberg mentioned may have been fresh in the minds of Soviet leaders during the Able Archer 83 exercises. One of them was the unusual public display of nuclear bellicosity on the part of William Dyess, Assistant Secretary of State for Public Information, in 1980 where he expanded on the newly proclaimed Carter Doctrine at a press conference:

Q: In nuclear war are we committed not to make the first strike?
Dyess: No sir.
Q: We could conceivably make an offensive . . .
Dyess: We make no comment on that whatsoever, but the Soviets know that this terrible weapon has been dropped on human beings twice in history and it was an American president who dropped it both times. Therefore, they have to take this into consideration in their calculus.[11]

Later that year the Carter administration issued secret, explicit warnings to the Soviet Union over the massing of Soviet troops on the Iranian border.[12]

The Soviet Union was not the only country whose behavior may have been influenced by America's willingness to use nuclear weapons. Early on in the Korean War, Truman told a reporter that the use of the atomic bomb was under active consideration.[13]

Eisenhower also considered using the atomic bomb in North Korea. In 1961, Eisenhower's former chief of staff wrote in his memoirs that Eisenhower believed the armistice in Korea was reached because of the "danger of atomic war.... They didn't want a full-scale war or an atomic attack. That kept them under some control." John Foster Dulles, his secretary of state, corroborated that account.[14]

Ellsberg notes, "Whether such threats actually affected the Chinese decision makers or whether they even received them remains uncertain and controversial." But there is little doubt that such aggressive threats were an integral part of America's approach to international affairs. Dulles was quite clear about the matter, describing an approach to nuclear diplomacy that became known as "brinkmanship."

> Some say that we were brought to the verge of war. Of course we were brought to the verge of war.... The ability to get to the verge without getting into the war is the necessary art. If you cannot master it, you inevitably get into war. If you try to run away from it, if you are scared to go the brink, you are lost.[15]

Of course, even brinkmanship has its subtleties. It is one thing to threaten the Russians with a tactical nuclear attack. They would know that the United States would have to take Russia's strategic nuclear capabilities into account. But all a country without nuclear weapons could hope for in such a situation would be that a strategic nuclear power such as Russia or China would back them up—a slender reed at best. For countries that already feel they are in America's crosshairs, developing their own deterrents may seem like the best option.

North Korea may be such a nation. There is no question that all three postwar leaders of North Korea—Kim Il Sung, Kim Jong Il, and Kim Jong Un—father, son, and grandson—have all been brutal dictators. But it would be a mistake to conclude that the nuclear weapons program of the current leader, Kim Jong Un, is irrational. He is almost certainly aware the United States was prepared to explode atomic bombs over his grandfather's country during the Korean War. He also knows the United States renewed this threat against his father in 1995 over North Korea's first nuclear power plant.[16]

So, while it may seem odd to some people that Kim is trying nuclear intimidation against the United States when any attack by him would almost certainly lead to the annihilation of his country, it may be a perfectly rational move.

Kim may simply be following the lead of China, the world's third-largest nuclear power. Although the Chinese maintain a substantial nuclear force, it is small enough that a potential adversary would view it only as a deterrent rather than one capable of launching a preemptive first strike.[17]

Kim is quite likely trying to acquire just enough of a nuclear strike force that it would make the United States think twice about issuing nuclear threats against North Korea. The U.S. may not want to risk a tit-for-tat exchange in which a "tactical" nuclear attack against Korea could lead to the disappearance of Silicon Valley in response.

Given the behavior of the United States, Gar Alperovitz's notion of atomic diplomacy looks very different in the light of events since 1945 than it does if one examines only events that occurred before Hiroshima. One can choose either Roosevelt's language, that the United States has served as the "police," or Churchill's, that it has carried out a policy of "international blackmail." In either case, the U.S. has engaged in what today one might call "open carry." The gun has not been in our pocket, as James Byrnes would have had it in his dealings with the Soviet Union immediately after the war. Rather, it has been ostentatiously hanging from our hip, and we have been more than willing to brandish it about.

One did not have to be deeply enmeshed in the intricacies of international relations to realize this a long time ago. In his classic study of 1956, *The Power Elite*, the sociologist C. Wright Mills recognized that "in the higher circles there has been a replacement of diplomacy in any historically recognized sense by calculations of war potential and the military seriousness of war threats. . . . The only seriously accepted plan for 'peace' is the fully loaded pistol."[18]

Unfortunately, we may have ended up pointing the pistol at our own head rather than at someone else's. In a 2018 article in *Harper's Magazine*, Andrew Cockburn reviewed some of the vagaries of the Pentagon's strategic "launch on attack" system. What Cockburn described is very much like Daniel Ellsberg's earlier account of how a few renegade officers in a missile silo could launch their weapon without authorization from a higher authority. And, as in Ellsberg's account, those higher authorities have not been particularly motivated to change the situation.

The reason for their reluctance is also pretty much the same. Cockburn quotes Lee Butler, the commander of all U.S. nuclear forces at the end of the Cold War. The military's decision-making process is "structured to drive the president invariably toward a decision to launch under attack" if there appears to be "incontrovertible proof that warheads actually are on the way." Structuring the system in this way is known as "'jamming' the president." Launching America's missiles and bombers before any enemy missiles landed would ensure "that most of the targets in the strategic nuclear war plan would be destroyed—thereby justifying the purchase and deployment of the massive force required to execute such a strike."[19]

Until the administration of George W. Bush, the alerts raised by the early detection systems were all handled at levels below the president. For example, when Jimmy Carter's national security advisor "was awakened at three in the morning in 1979 by what turned out to be a false alarm regarding incoming Soviet missiles, the president learned what had happened only the following day." Throughout the Cold War and for a decade after it ended, there was enough of what one might call "room" in the system that no president had to make the decision to launch or not launch. Nor was the president "jammed" toward the desired outcome. "Today, things are different," Cockburn tells us. "The nuclear fuse has gotten shorter."[20]

What initially seemed to be a mere change in fortune for one side in the constant Pentagon battles over budgets has led to an ominous difference in the handling of nuclear alerts. In the past, the initial warnings of a possible attack went through the National Military Command Center, which is directed by a one-star general. Moreover, the officers actually in charge were lowly colonels and "therefore . . . reluctant to disturb or wake the commander in chief for what could be a false alarm." But the initial warnings of an attack now go to a four-star air force general, who commands the entire U.S. strategic arsenal otherwise known as STRATCOM. In 2018 the STRATCOM commander was General John Hyten.

Four-star generals, Cockburn points out, "are the gods of the military hierarchy, accustomed to deference from all around them. Such panjandrums, especially those with the means to end human civilization, can be expected to have fewer inhibitions against disturbing presidential slumbers." As a result, both Bush and Obama received several "urgent calls," and Trump and Biden probably did as well. "Thus," Cockburn tells us, "in a real or apparent crisis the crucial and necessarily fraught conversation may be between two men: General Hyten and [the president]."[21]

To make matters still more vexing, the modernization of nuclear weapons is continuing on all sides. The Russians, for example, have developed highly maneuverable "hypersonic" cruise missiles that are much harder for traditional warning and alert systems to track.

General Hyten offered assurances at a security conference that he would not obey a capricious order by Trump to launch a first-strike attack. "The way the process works is this simple: I provide advice to the president. He'll tell me what to do, and if it's illegal . . . I'm going to say, 'Mr. President, it's illegal.'"[22]

Unfortunately, Hyten might not have an opportunity to override a presidential order to launch. Once the president executes the launch codes carried by a military aide who is always by his side, the general will see the order at the same time as the officers at the command centers who carry it out.

CHAPTER 19

Tickling the Dragon's Tail

Nuclear weapons seem to have an allure like no weapon before them. The physicist Freeman Dyson suggested:

[They] have a glitter more seductive than gold to those who play with them. To command nature to release in a pint pot the energy that fuels the stars, to lift by pure thought a million tons of rock into the sky, these are exercises of the human will that produce an illusion of illimitable power.[1]

Clearly, it's not just scientists who are affected by fantasies of illimitable power. Politicians are as well. In politics, the attraction can be for purposes grandiose or petty. It can stem from a quest for personal power on a grand scale or allegiance to a nation, a political party, or an ideology; or it can simply be part of a political maneuver over budgeting.

An incident during the Manhattan Project can offer us a salutary lesson about what we may be doing to ourselves when we grasp at such dangerous illusions.

The essential engineering concept behind an atomic bomb is to create a lump of uranium or plutonium large enough to trigger an atomic chain reaction that results in a massive release of energy—a "critical mass." A major problem for anyone who wants to build a usable atomic bomb is that once the critical mass is reached, it will explode almost instantly. So instead, the bomb is constructed with two separate spheres, each equal to one half of the critical mass. The trigger of the bomb creates the atomic blast by setting off a carefully designed charge of conventional explosives that drives the two spheres together in perfect alignment.

During the Manhattan Project, the research sometimes required physicists to experiment with the two spheres, bringing them close but not completely together in tests of "near criticality." Such tests are dangerous, a form of laboratory brinkmanship. Physicists at the Manhattan Project called them "tickling the dragon's tail."[2]

If the spheres of an atomic bomb are brought too close together, they could release a deadly dose of radiation. That is exactly what happened to two experimenters, Harry Daghlian and Louis Slotin. On two separate occasions, the spheres accidentally slipped from their control, giving each of them a fatal dose of radiation.[3]

Illusionary or not, it is easy to see that the prospect of illimitable power is often a seductive attraction regardless of the danger. Perhaps it is the case that for many of the scientists at the Manhattan Project, the thrill of discovery and a sense of intimacy with the forces of nature was sufficient. But even then, they seemed to have taken a cavalier attitude toward the forces they were unleashing.

During the early stages of the bomb's development Oppenheimer and Edward Teller calculated that the atomic bomb might trigger a fusion reaction capable of "setting afire the atmosphere of the entire planet."[4] They held up work on the bomb until they had determined that their initial calculations had overestimated the likelihood of such a catastrophic event. They decided that the chance of such a devastating reaction was only three in a million, although that number was more of a seat-of-the-pants approximation than the result of a hard-and-fast calculation.

Oppenheimer's boss, the physicist Arthur Compton, decided such a risk was "low enough to be worth taking." However, it is not clear from the historical record if that conclusion was reached by a consensus of those involved or if "the physicists hemmed and hawed a long time" before the figure was set at Compton's orders.[5] One project leader at the Manhattan Project recalled, "It was by no means certain . . . The doubts continued still in 1945. . . . We weren't supposed to tell the younger people. They kept making the discovery for themselves and coming to warn us."[6]

The possibility of ultimate and total destruction still lingered to the extent that one of the most prominent physicists on the project, Enrico Fermi, invited bets "against first the destruction of all human life and second just that of human life in New Mexico." Leslie Groves, who was at the meeting, "decided that Fermi was merely making a bad joke out of a desire to relieve tension. A good many of the senior physicists present felt that Fermi was not merely joking."[7]

Despite the scientists' unease about the possible consequences of their work, no one in charge in New Mexico seemed to think that possibility was something officials in Washington should know about. After all, by the time the bets were being taken at Alamogordo, the war in Germany was over and there would be no Nazi bomb. The attraction of illimitable power through the control of the fundamental forces of nature may have created a momentum of its own among scientists far removed from the deliberations over invasions or postwar diplomacy.

Politicians and military leaders, on the other hand, are far more interested in power over other people than in understanding the forces of nature. The lure of the bomb is what led Roosevelt to modify his idea that the most powerful nations would become the Policemen of the world. With the atomic bomb, there need be only one Policeman on the beat: the United States. He was no more interested in the forces of nature behind the bomb than an ordinary policeman is in the physics of the gun he carries on his belt.

Roosevelt's decision to grasp at illimitable power helped set in motion a chain reaction of its own, one that has cast a shadow over human life the world over. Even leading American nuclear strategists have sometimes expressed a sense of foreboding over the way illimitable power over nature seemed to be leading to uncontrollable chaos. George Kennan, perhaps the most prominent architect of America's policy in the Cold War, wondered, "Are we to flee like haunted creatures from one defensive device to another, each more costly and humiliating than the one before, cowering underground one day, breaking up our cities the next, attempting to surround ourselves with elaborate shields on the third . . . ?"[8]

Of course, countries that lacked nuclear weapons did not have the luxury of indulging in such musings. Their options were to seek an alliance with an existing nuclear power, attempt to build their own nuclear weapons in the face of threats and reprisals from existing nuclear powers, or simply cower. As the possible global atmospheric effects of even a "limited" nuclear war became better known, it also became apparent that nonnuclear countries could face annihilation as the result of a nuclear war in which they were not even participants.[9]

The chain reaction in human affairs also profoundly affected the government of the United States. Leslie Groves's attempts to influence nuclear policy is an early example. Bureaucrats follow the leader, but they do so in their own way and often according to their own agendas. President Truman and his secretary of war approved of Groves's attempts to control uranium, but they did not authorize him to leak reports of dubious veracity about Soviet spying to the press or to secretly lobby Congress regarding the control of nuclear weapons. Yet that lobbying by a brigadier general, a relatively lowly position in the larger structure of governmental power, undermined Truman's own policies.

It is all too easy to view Groves's behavior as an aberration, a gross departure from the normal behavior of government workers both military and civilian. But that is not necessarily the case. For example, Daniel Ellsberg described an instance in which the Pentagon refused to honor a request from the president for a copy of its operational plan for nuclear war.[10] In another instance, an admiral lied to the Defense Department about the presence of atomic weapons in Japanese waters—weapons that were in direct violation of the United States' agreements with Japan.[11] The secretary of defense let those transgressions pass because, Ellsberg suggests, "McNamara had to pick his fights."[12]

The kind of bureaucratic infighting Ellsberg describes has probably been going on for as long as there have been social hierarchies. As Graham Allison and Philip Zelikow explain in their classic study, *Essence of Decision: Explaining the Cuban Missile Crisis*, these are examples of a much broader set of issues that affect how governmental power is exercised.

As their title suggests, Allison and Zelikow use the historical record of the Cuban Missile Crisis as a case study. Their study shows how organizational complexity in and of itself can lead to a loss of control over governmental behavior, including the use of nuclear weapons. And yet bureaucracies are necessary for complex undertakings of all kinds, including collecting taxes, maintaining interstate transportation systems such as interstate highways and air travel, overseeing environmental laws, and countless other functions. Military affairs and international relations are among the most complex and difficult to control.

Allison and Zelikow describe three ways of looking at decision-making in foreign and military affairs. They begin with a fairly standard description of the Cuban Missile Crisis in terms of what they call the Rational Actor Model. Under this model, analysts "attempt to understand happenings in foreign affairs as the more or less purposive acts of unified national governments." The Rational Actor Model focuses on the strategic problems each country faces and analyzes its behavior in terms of its goals and objectives.[13] The authors describe how an analyst working under the Rational Actor Model would "frame the puzzle" in examining the Cuban Missile Crisis:

Why did the Soviet Union decide to install missiles in Cuba? He focuses attention on . . . goals and objectives of the nation or government. . . . The analyst has "explained" this event when he can show how placing missiles in Cuba was a reasonable action, given Soviet strategic objectives. Predictions about what a nation will do or would have done are generated by calculating the rational thing to do in a certain situation, given specified objectives.[14]

Of course, a more detailed account, like Ellsberg's, would tell us what President Kennedy and Khrushchev and their respective advisors decided to do at each stage of the crisis, along with the various factors they had to consider. They would view those factors in terms of how they affect "strategic goals" which serve "national security and national interests." They would evaluate alternative courses of action in terms of the "benefits and costs" they might engender. Thus, under the Rational Actor Model, their decisions would be assumed to be their attempt at "value-maximizing" in an "international strategic 'marketplace.'"[15]

If this sounds a lot like the economic framework encountered with Albert Wohlstetter's cost–benefit approach to the Vietnam War, it is because the Rational Actor Model was initially developed by an economist, Thomas Schelling.[16] As Allison and Zelikow explain, in economics, rational consumers buy the things that best meet their needs at the lowest cost they can find while companies try to maximize their profits in producing those goods. Under the Rational Actor Model, nations do something similar. They try to get as much as they want while avoiding unpleasant consequences as much as they can. The model conceives of the behavior of nations in much the same way economists view the behavior of consumers and factory owners: they are all trying to "maximize utility."

It is fairly easy to frame Ellsberg's description of the Cuban crisis in these terms. For example, early on, McNamara characterized the presence of atomic weapons in Cuba as a domestic political problem rather than a military one. Some of Kennedy's advisors weren't so sure. For one thing, allowing the missiles to remain in Cuba would incur a severe cost in the "international strategic marketplace" with regard to the United States' overall strategic position with its European allies regarding Berlin. Moreover, the domestic political costs might have been extremely high, not just for the Kennedy administration, but for future presidents as well.

They gathered as much information as they could about the Soviet Union's military position in Cuba. They then decided they could threaten Khrushchev because they believed the Soviets had more to lose in a military conflict in Cuba than the United States did.

Allison and Zelikow don't claim the Rational Actor Model is wrong, only that it is incomplete. They offer two other models of decision-making. They call their second model the Organizational Model. Under this perspective,

> a government is not an individual. It is not just the president and his entourage, nor even just the presidency and Congress. It is a vast conglomerate of loosely allied organizations, each with a substantial life of its own. . . . These organizations enact routines. Governmental behaviors can therefore be understood . . . less as deliberate choices and more as *outputs* [italics in the original] of large organizations functioning according to standard patterns of behavior.[17]

One example Allison and Zelikow give has to do with the physical structure of the missile bases the Soviets installed in Cuba. The bases conformed to the same physical pattern the Americans had observed in their surveillance flights over missile bases in the Soviet Union. The Soviets were aware of this surveillance, yet they built the bases the exact same way in Cuba, making it easy for American analysts to recognize them almost immediately. The Soviets did not even try to camouflage them.

Allison and Zelikow point out that this was the first time the missiles had been installed outside of the Soviet Union. So when the installation teams were told to get the missiles in place ready for use as quickly as possible, "each team did what it knew how to do—emplace missiles—literally according to the book." They didn't have time to experiment with untried physical configurations or procedures that might or might not have resulted in missiles that were operational by the date their orders specified. They didn't attempt to camouflage the missiles for similar reasons. They had never attempted it in the Soviet Union, and trying to do so would have added time and complexity.[18]

They did take steps to conceal the missile sites once they had been set up, but by that time, the United States had already learned the Soviets were moving ballistic missiles into Cuba. Allison and Zelikow suggest,

> An intelligence agency would likely have made a different choice, but a field organization in the business of deploying missiles could be expected to focus first on completion of preparation for possible combat, particularly when that directive came with a date attached. Thus the troops in the missile regiments did what they knew how to do, sometimes to the point of exhaustion.[19]

A similar process may have been at work with the problem Daniel Ellsberg discovered regarding the delegation of authority whereby local commanders who lost contact with their superiors were authorized to launch a nuclear attack on their own. The logic of delegation is clear enough, and such an arrangement may have made sense in a conventional war where a mistaken assumption may have led to a conventional military defeat. But no one seems to have questioned such an arrangement in the nuclear age, when an uninformed decision can put the continued existence of human life on earth at risk.

Even more alarming is the problem Ellsberg discovered with the F-100 tactical fighter-bombers at the forward bases in the Eastern Pacific. These were the planes armed with nuclear bombs designed to be carried inside the body of the aircraft, but because the planes did not have enough room internally, the bombs were mounted externally, greatly increasing the danger of an accidental explosion.

The Pentagon likely assigned the planes to those bases because they were the best match for the mission. Funding, designing, and building a plane more suited to the task would have taken years. The commanders at the bases adapted standard procedures to fit the situation as best they could. As a result, the decision to start a nuclear war could have devolved to the pilot of a single fighter-bomber.

Allison and Zelikow call their third model the Governmental Politics Model. Anyone who has ever been in a meeting with people who had to make a decision, whether at work, at a church, or in a community group, knows that reaching an agreement is not a simple matter.

In governments, there can be dozens of meetings across different governmental organizations. The decisions made in those meetings are the result of negotiations between and within the various organizations that make up the government. Those decisions might deal with coordination between the State Department and the Defense Department regarding foreign military bases, relationships with NATO, and other military alliances. Various intelligence agencies from different parts of the government are also involved in diplomatic and military decision-making. Each of those groups has a director or cabinet officer in charge, and below them are subgroups, each with their own hierarchies, in a seemingly endless regression.

The "rational actors" at the top base their decisions on the information coming to them from below. At each stage, the conclusions can be colored, changed, or even reversed, depending on the institutional and personal dynamics of those sitting around those departmental conference tables. As we have already seen, the battles over Reagan's Star Wars provide a good example.

Alarmed by a report from the CIA that the Soviet Union had sharply reduced its spending on nuclear weapons once it had reached parity with the United States, Robert Gates and Caspar Weinberger suppressed the report because it undermined their position in their battles with the State Department over the value of arms control versus the continuation of an aggressive military buildup by the United States.

A similar process may have been at work during World War II regarding Japanese culture and society. One commonly held assumption about the Japanese was that they were ferociously determined to fight regardless of the circumstances. As one journalist observed, "Psychological warfare seldom was employed against the Japanese, who were regarded popularly as too inhuman to be propagandized."[20]

As early as April 1944, a group of social scientists at the Foreign Morale Division of the Office of War Information concluded that such commonly held assumptions were incorrect. After examining captured diaries and studying the behavior of Japanese prisoners of war, the scientists concluded that a psychological warfare campaign directed at Japan's soldiers, leaders, and civilian population would likely increase battlefield surrenders and possibly bring about an earlier end to the war.

In January of 1945 the Division issued another report describing clear evidence of defeatism and social disintegration in the Japanese homeland. The social scientists advocated a psychological warfare program, offering reassurance that the imperial system would be preserved and innocent citizens left in peace.

For the American people and within government itself, such proposals undermined an important justification for pursuing total surrender. One of the arguments Secretary of War Stimson made for using the atomic bomb was that there was no indication the Japanese determination to continue fighting was weakening. But the higher officials at the Office of War Information refused to pass the report to those in policy-making positions, so Stimson was relying on incomplete information. One of the social scientists commented "The administrator uses social science the way a drunk uses a lamppost, for support rather than for illumination."[21]

Both the Organizational Model and the Governmental Politics Model undermine many of the assumptions behind the Rational Actor Model. The notion that the leaders of a nation-state are acting in a rational manner is difficult to accept when the internal processes of their own government are likely to distort their understanding of the situation with which they are attempting to deal.

The Rational Actor Model may be useful for analyzing the behavior of the leaders of nation-states before 1945, but in the nuclear era, the stakes are no longer the destruction of an army, the sacking of a city, or the fall of an empire. In the nuclear era, when annihilation of humanity itself is the likely outcome for failure to navigate what one might call the "fog of brinkmanship," such thinking is anything but rational.

Nikita Khrushchev may have been the first leader to fully understand this. When Robert Kennedy threatened a full-scale military attack against Cuba if there were any more attempts to shoot down American reconnaissance planes, the Soviet leader knew two critical facts the Americans were not aware of. First, Khrushchev could not control whether or not the Cubans would shoot at American planes flying over the island. Second, many tactical nuclear weapons had been deployed in Cuba, and the Cubans' decision to use them in the event of an American attack was also beyond his control. He realized the possibility of an ultimate "negative outcome" for both sides was far greater than the Americans understood, and he decided to "maximize" everybody's "utility" by withdrawing the missiles.

One could view physicist Leo Szilard's visit with Secretary of State Byrnes in late May 1945 as an implicit clash of the nuclear and prenuclear modes of rationality. This was the meeting where Szilard told Byrnes the United States should stop development of the atomic bomb and let the Russians think the American attempt to build the bomb had failed.

It is hard to know how American diplomats would have viewed the Soviet Union's military situation in Europe at the end of World War II if the atomic bomb had never been developed. They may have tried other means of reaching an accommodation with Stalin. More voices in the bureaucracy may have suggested that protecting his borders was Stalin's primary goal. After all, at one point, Roosevelt saw the Soviet Union as one of the Four Policemen that would constitute a global police force.

The fear of a possible Soviet invasion of Western Europe would likely have been a factor in any case. However, after the loss of at least twenty million soldiers and civilians in the war, it is unlikely that Stalin was eager to launch an assault on Western Europe in the near future. A modest number of American troops in Europe might have been enough to convince him to stay within the territory he already controlled. The United States could have then helped its European allies rebuild their own conventional military forces as quickly as possible.

Relying on atomic weapons was a cheap way for the United States to avoid the expense of creating such a deterrent, but only if one were willing to ignore the warnings from the people who were actually building the bomb that using it could lead to an arms race. Truman and Byrnes chose to ignore those warnings and insisted that America's atomic monopoly would last indefinitely.

When the three prime contractors on the Manhattan Project—Dupont, Union Carbide, and Eastman—warned Byrnes that the Russians could build a bomb in five years, Byrnes chose instead to rely on General Groves's assertion that America's atomic monopoly could last as long as two decades, despite the fact that Groves knew virtually nothing about the technical requirements for building an atomic bomb. And after the war Truman and Byrnes allowed the philanthropist Bernard Baruch, who proudly declared that all he wanted to know about the atomic bomb was that it killed millions of people, to set his contentious postwar atomic policy toward Russia.

Most puzzling of all was Truman himself. He understood that the science and engineering knowledge to build an atomic bomb was well within the reach of other nations. Yet he clung to the notion that somehow what he called the "combination of industrial capacity and resources necessary to produce the bomb" would be beyond the reach of other nations for the foreseeable future.

Truman's decision to disregard the warnings about an arms race may have been due, at least in part, to the fact that when he assumed office in May 1945, America's nuclear trajectory had already been set by Roosevelt. Professor Robert A. Divine noted, "Roosevelt's concept of big power domination remained the central idea in his approach to international organization throughout World War II."[22] At first Roosevelt envisioned needing partners in order to maintain that domination. But the lure of illimitable power led him to change his thinking. His actions suggest that he intended to take full advantage of the bomb's potential as a postwar instrument of Anglo-American diplomacy. If Roosevelt thought the bomb could be used to create a more peaceful world order, he seems to have considered the threat of its power more effective than any opportunities it offered for international cooperation.

It's clear that Roosevelt contemplated how other nations might react when "Manhattan appears over their homeland" well before Truman did.

When the time came to assemble the bomb for the first test at Alamogordo, General Groves sent a young military officer named Thomas Farrell to represent him. Louis Slotin (one of the physicists who later died "tickling the dragon's tail") placed the two hemi-spheres of the bomb inside a capsule. The capsule would become a functional bomb once an "intricately carved" shaped charge of gunpowder was inserted, driving the two hemispheres together to create a critical mass.

> Slotin pointed to the capsule and told Farrell to touch it. . . . Surprised to see it so small, Farrell put his hands on it . . . and felt the thing was warm. At some point in the higher levels of his nervous system, he recalled later, the sensation turned into a thrill of realization and dread.[23]

Indeed, we must let the dread reach the higher levels of our nervous systems. The dragon might soon twitch its tail.

ABOUT THE AUTHOR

JEFFREY L. KAPLAN's articles on American history have appeared in *Sustainability: A Bedford Spotlight Reader*, a college reader published by Bedford/St. Martin's; *Poverty & Race in America: The Emerging Agendas*, Rowman & Littlefield; and *The Future of Nature: Writing on a Human Ecology*, Milkweed Editions.

BIBLIOGRAPHY

Albright, Madeleine. "Punishing Saddam." Interview by *60 Minutes*, May 12, 1996. https://www.youtube.com/watch?v=RM0uvgHKZe8.

Albright, Madeleine. Interview by Matt Lauer. *The Today Show*, February 19, 1998. https://1997-2001.state.gov/statements/1998/980219a.html.

Allison, Graham, and Philip Zelikow. *Essence of Decision: Explaining the Cuban Missile Crisis*. 2nd ed. New York: Longman, 1999.

Alperovitz, Gar. *Atomic Diplomacy: Hiroshima and Potsdam*. New York: Pluto Press, 1994.

Alperovitz, Gar. *The Decision to Use the Atomic Bomb*. New York: Vintage 1996.

American Society of Civil Engineers (ASCE). *Report Card for America's Infrastructure*. Accessed 12/03/2024: ASCE, 2021. https://infrastructurereportcard.org/wp-content/uploads/2020/12/National_IRC_2021-report.pdf.

Atomic Heritage Foundation. "Reagan and Gorbachev: The Geneva Summit." Atomic Heritage Foundation. July 26, 2018. https://www.atomicheritage.org/history/reagan-and-gorbachev-geneva-summit.

Atomic Heritage Foundation. "Smyth Report." Atomic Heritage Foundation. Accessed 12-03-2024. https://www.atomicheritage.org/key-documents/smyth-report.

Bacevich, Andrew J. *Limits of Power: The End of American Exceptionalism*. New York: Holt, 2008.

Bibliography

Bacevich, Andrew J. *The New American Militarism: How Americans Are Seduced by War*. New York: Oxford University Press, 2013.

Becker, Jo, and Scott Shane. "Secret 'Kill List' Proves a Test of Obama's Principles and Will." https://www.nytimes.com/2012/05/29/world/obamas-leadership-in-war-on-al-qaeda.html.

Bernstein, Barton J. "Roosevelt, Truman, and the Atomic Bomb, 1941-1945: A Reinterpretation." *Political Science Quarterly* 90, no. 1 (Spring 1975): 23–69.

Bernstein, Barton J. "Perils and Politics of Surrender: Ending the War with Japan and Avoiding the Third Atomic Bomb." *Pacific Historical Review* 46, no. 1 (February 1977).

Bernstein, Barton J. "The Atomic Bombings Reconsidered." *Foreign Affairs* 74, no. 1 (1995): 135–152.

Bernstein, Barton J. "Introducing the Interpretive Problems of Japan's 1945 Surrender: A Historiographical Essay on Recent Literature in the West." In *The End of the Pacific War*, edited by Tsuyoshi Hasegawa, 9–64. Stanford, CA: Stanford University Press, 2007.

Blanton, Thomas. "Annals of Blinksmanship." *Wilson Quarterly*, 1997. https://nsarchive2.gwu.edu/nsa/cuba_mis_cri/annals.htm.

Boyer, Paul. *By the Bomb's Early Light: American Thought and Culture at the Dawn of the Atomic Age*. Chapel Hill: University of North Carolina Press, 1994.

Brennan, John O. "Efficacy and Ethics of U.S. Counterterrorism Strategy." Wilson Center, April 30, 2012. https://www.wilsoncenter.org/event/the-efficacy-and-ethics-us-counterterrorism-strategy.

Burr, William, and Thomas S. Blanton, eds. "The Submarines of October U.S. and Soviet Naval Encounters during the Cuban Missile Crisis." National

Bibliography

Security Archive Electronic Briefing Book No. 75, October 31, 2002. https://nsarchive2.gwu.edu/NSAEBB/NSAEBB75/.

Bush, Vannevar. *Science, the Endless Frontier: A Report to the President on a Program for Postwar Scientific Research.* Washington, DC: United States Government Printing Office, 1945.

Bush, Vannevar. *Endless Horizons.* Washington, DC: Public Affairs Press, 1946.

Butler, Susan. *Roosevelt and Stalin: Portrait of a Partnership.* New York: Alfred A. Knopf, 2015.

Calleo, David P. *Follies of Power: America's Unipolar Fantasy.* Cambridge: Cambridge University Press, 2009.

Carter, Jimmy. "Crisis of Confidence." The Carter Center, July 14, 1979. https://www.cartercenter.org/news/editorials_speeches/crisis_of_confidence.html.

Carter, Jimmy. "State of the Union Address 1980." Jimmy Carter Library. Accessed 12-03-2024. https://www.jimmycarterlibrary.gov/the-carters/selected-speeches/jimmy-carter-state-of-the-union-address-1980.

Chomsky, Noam. "Rollback - Part I." *Z Magazine*, January 1995. Accessed January 5, 2025. https://thirdworldtraveler.com/Chomsky/Rollback_Part1_Chom.html.

Cockburn, Alexander. "How to Start a Nuclear War: The Increasing Direct Road to Ruin." *Harper's Magazine*, August 2018.

"James Madison: Birthday Quotes from the Most Quotable Founding Father." National Constitution Center. March 16, 2016. https://constitutioncenter.org/blog/james-madison-birthday-quotes-from-the-most-quotable-founding-father.

Bibliography

Correll, John T. "They Called It Star Wars: The Critics Sneered at It, but the Soviets Weren't So Sure." *Air Force Magazine*, June 2012. https://www.airforcemag.com/PDF/MagazineArchive/Documents/2012/June%20 2012/0612starwars.pdf.

Cray, Ed. *General of the Army: George C. Marshall, Soldier and Statesman.* New York: Cooper Square Press, 2000.

Davis, Nuel Pharr. *Lawrence and Oppenheimer.* New York: Simon & Schuster, 1968.

Debs, Alexandre, and Nuno P. Monteiro. *Nuclear Politics: The Strategic Causes of Proliferation.* Cambridge: Cambridge University Press, 2017.

Dickson, David. *The New Politics of Science.* Chicago: University of Chicago Press, 1988.

Dobbs, Michael. *One Minute to Midnight: Kennedy, Khrushchev, and Castro on the Brink of Nuclear War.* New York: Vintage, 2009.

Dower, John W. *War without Mercy: Race & Power in the Pacific War.* New York: Pantheon Books, 1986.

Durbin, Brent. "Bureaucratic Politics Approach." Britannica. Accessed 12-03-2024. https://www.britannica.com/topic/bureaucratic-politics-approach#ref1181380.

Dyson, Freeman. *Disturbing the Universe.* New York: Harper & Row, 1981.

Ellsberg, Daniel. *The Doomsday Machine: Confessions of a Nuclear War Planner.* New York: Bloomsbury, 2017.

FitzGerald, Frances. *Way Out There in the Blue: Reagan, Star Wars and the End of the Cold War.* New York: Simon & Schuster, 2000.

Frank, Richard B. *Downfall: The End of the Imperial Japanese Empire.* New York: Random House, 1999.

Bibliography

Frank, Richard B. "Ketsu Gō: Japanese Political and Military Strategy in 1945." In *The End of the Pacific War*, edited by Tsuyoshi Hasegawa, 65–94. Stanford, CA: Stanford University Press, 2007.

Freedman, Lawrence D. "After the Cold War." Britannica. Accessed November 25, 2024. https://www.britannica.com/topic/nuclear-strategy/After-the-Cold-War.

Friedersdorf, Connor. "The Obama Administration's Drone-Strike Dissembling." *Atlantic*, March 14, 2016. https://www.theatlantic.com/politics/archive/2016/03/the-obama-administrations-drone-strike-dissembling/473541/.

Friedman, Thomas. "A Manifesto for the Fast World." *New York Times*, March 28, 1999. https://www.nytimes.com/1999/03/28/magazine/a-manifesto-for-the-fast-world.html.

Gaddis, John Lewis. *The United States and the Origins of the Cold War*. New York: Columbia University Press, 2000.

Gentile, Gian P. *How Effective Is Strategic Bombing? Lessons Learned from World War II to Kosovo*. New York: New York University Press, 2001.

Global Policy Forum. "Iraq Sanctions: Humanitarian Implications and Options for the Future." Global Policy Forum, August 6, 2002. https://www.globalpolicy.org/component/content/article/170/41947.html.

Gorbachev, Mikhail. *Political Report of the CPSU Central Committee to the 27th Party Congress*. Moscow: Novosti Press Agency Publishing House, 1986. https://archive.org/details/PoliticalReportOfTheCPSUCentralCommitteeToThe27thPartyCongress/page/n5.

Harbutt, Fraser J. *Yalta 1945: Europe and America at the Crossroads*. Cambridge: Cambridge University Press, 2010.

Bibliography

Harvard Pusey Library. "Where Disaster Strikes: Modern Space and the Visualization of Destruction." Harvard Map Collection. Accessed November 23, 2024. https://blogs.harvard.edu/wheredisasterstrikes/war/warsaw-1939/.

Hasegawa, Tsuyoshi. *Racing the Enemy: Stalin, Truman, and the Surrender of Japan*. Cambridge, MA: Harvard University Press, 2005.

Hasegawa, Tsuyoshi. "The Atomic Bomb and the Soviet Invasion: Which Was More Important in Japan's Decision to Surrender?" In *The End of the Pacific War*, edited by Tsuyoshi Hasegawa, 113–144. Stanford, CA: Stanford University Press, 2007a.

Hasegawa, Tsuyoshi. *The End of the Pacific War: Reappraisals*. Stanford, CA: Stanford University Press, 2007b.

Hasegawa, Tsuyoshi. "The Soviet Factor in Ending the Pacific War: From the Neutrality Pact to Soviet Entry into the War in August 1945." In *The End of the Pacific War*, edited by Tsuyoshi Hasegawa, 202–227. Stanford, CA: Stanford University Press, 2007c.

Hasegawa, Tsuyoshi. "The Atomic Bombs and the Soviet Invasion." In *The End of the Pacific War*, edited by Tsuyoshi Hasegawa, 136. Stanford, CA: Stanford University Press, 2007c.

Hatano, Sumio. "The Atomic Bomb and Soviet Entry into the War: Of Equal Importance." In *The End of the Pacific War*, edited by Tsuyoshi Hasegawa, 95–112. Stanford, CA: Stanford University Press, 2007.

Herken, Gregg. *The Winning Weapon: The Atomic Bomb in the Cold War 1945–1950*. New York: Alfred A. Knopf, 1980.

Herken, Gregg. *Cardinal Choices: Presidential Science Advising from the Atomic Bomb to SDI*. Stanford, CA: Stanford University Press, 1992.

Hiltzik, Michael. *Big Science: Ernest Lawrence and the Invention That Launched the Military Industrial Complex*. New York: Simon & Schuster, 2015.

Bibliography

History Maps. 1973 Oil Crisis. Accessed December 3, 2024. https://history-maps.com/story/History-of-Saudi-Arabia/event/1973-Oil-Crisis. For gas prices, see also: https://afdc.energy.gov/data/10641.

Holloway, David. *Stalin and the Bomb*. New Haven and London: Yale University Press, 1994.

Jacobs, Meg. "America's Never-Ending Oil Consumption." *Atlantic*, May 16, 2016. https://www.theatlantic.com/politics/archive/2016/05/american-oil-consumption/482532/.

Jones, Nate. "The 1983 War Scare: 'The Last Paroxysm' of the Cold War Part II." National Security Archive, May 21, 2013. https://nsarchive2.gwu.edu/NSAEBB/NSAEBB427/.

Jones, Nate. "The 1983 War Scare: 'The Last Paroxysm' of the Cold War Part III." National Security Archive, May 22, 2013. https://nsarchive2.gwu.edu/NSAEBB/NSAEBB428/.

Jones, Nate, Tom Blanton, and Lauren Harper. "The 1983 War Scare Declassified and For Real." National Security Archive, October 24, 2015. https://nsarchive2.gwu.edu/nukevault/ebb533-The-Able-Archer-War-Scare-Declassified-PFIAB-Report-Released/.

Kennedy, John F. "Address During the Cuban Missile Crisis." October 22, 1962. https://www.jfklibrary.org/learn/about-jfk/historic-speeches/address-during-the-cuban-missile-crisis.

Kristensen, Hans M., Matt Korda, Eliana Johns, and Mackenzie Knight. "Chinese Nuclear Weapons, 2024." Bulletin of the Atomic Scientists 80 no. 1 (2024): https://doi.org/10.1080/00963402.2023.2295206.

Kristensen, Hans M., Matthew McKinzie, and Theodore A. Postol. "How US Nuclear Force Modernization is Undermining Strategic Stability: The Burst-Height Compensating Super-Fuze." *Bulletin of the Atomic Scientists* (March 1, 2017). https://thebulletin.org/2017/03/

how-us-nuclear-force-modernization-is-undermining-strategic-stability-the-burst-height-compensating-super-fuze/#.

Lockie, Alex. "We Ranked the World's Nuclear Arsenals—Here's Why China's Came out on Top." Business Insider, January 25, 2019. https://www.businessinsider.com/9-nuclear-nations-arsenals-ranked-us-vs-russia-china-wins-2019-1.

MacEachin, Douglas J. "The Final Months of the War with Japan." Central Intelligence Agency. Accessed November 25, 2024. https://www.cia.gov/resources/csi/static/The-Final-Months-of-the-War-With-Japan-Monograph.pdf.

MacIsaac, David. *Strategic Bombing in World War Two: The Story of the United States Strategic Bombing Survey.* New York: Garland Publishing, 1976.

Mastny, Vojtech. *Russia's Road to the Cold War.* New York: Columbia University Press, 1979.

McNamara, Robert S. *The Fog of War.* Directed by Errol Morris. Sony Pictures Classics, 2003. Factual America, September 5, 2024. https://www.factualamerica.com/history-revisited/9-tense-documentaries-about-the-cuban-missile-crisis..

Messer, Robert L. *The End of an Alliance: James F. Byrnes, Roosevelt, Truman, and the Origins of the Cold War.* New York: University of North Carolina Press, 1982.

Messer, Robert L. "New Evidence on Truman's Decision." In *A History of Our Time*, edited by William Henry Chafe and Harvard Sitkoff, 9–21. New York: Oxford University Press, 1995.

Mills, C. Wright, and Alan Wolfe. *The Power Elite: New Edition.* Oxford: Oxford University Press, 2000.

Bibliography

Mosher, Dave. "If India and Pakistan Have a 'Limited' Nuclear War, Scientists Say It Could Wreck Earth's Climate and Trigger Global Famine." Business Insider, February 28, 2019. https://www. businessinsider.com/india-pakistan-kashmir-nuclear-weapons-climate-cooling-2019-2.

Nagy, Thomas J. "The Role of 'Iraq Water Treatment Vulnerabilities' in Halting One Genocide and Preventing Others." George Washington University, June 12, 2001. http://www.casi.org.uk/info/nagy010612.pdf.

National Priorities Project. "The Militarized Budget 2020." https://www. nationalpriorities.org/analysis/2020/militarized-budget-2020/.

Nuclear Weapons Freeze Campaign. "Call to Halt the Nuclear Arms Race." 1981. https://livingwiththebomb.files.wordpress.com/2013/08/call-to-halt-arms-race.pdf.

Office of the Historian. "Foreign Relations of the United States: Diplomatic Papers, 1945, the Far East, China, Volume VII," Nanking Embassy Files, Lot F–73: Telegram. Accessed January 1, 2025. https://history.state.gov/historicaldocuments/frus1945v07/d348.

Orlov, Vadim. "Recollections of Vadim Orlov (USSR Submarine B-59), We Will Sink Them All, But We Will Not Disgrace Our Navy." Accessed November 20, 2024. https://nsarchive2.gwu.edu/NSAEBB/NSAEBB75/asw-II-16.pdf

Paltrow, Scott. "Special Report: In Modernizing Nuclear Arsenal, U.S. Stokes New Arms Race." Reuters, November 21, 2017. https://www. reuters.com/article/us-usa-nuclear-modernize-specialreport/special-report-in-modernizing-nuclear-arsenal-u-s-stokes-new-arms-race-idUSKBN1DL1AH.

Perkovich, George. "The Other Terrifying Lesson of the Cuban Missile Crisis." Politico, January 4, 2018. https://www.politico.com/magazine/

story/2018/01/04/the-other-terrifying-lesson-of-the-cuban-missile-crisis-216240.

Plokhy, S. M. *Yalta: The Price of Peace*. New York: Viking, 2010.

Podvig, Pavel. "Did Star Wars Help End the Cold War? Soviet Response to the SDI." Program Russian Nuclear Forces Project working paper, March 17, 2013. http://russianforces.org/podvig/2013/03/did_star_wars_help_end_the_col.html.

Podvig, Pavel. "Shooting Down the Star Wars Myth." Bulletin of the Atomic Scientists, April 30, 2013. https://thebulletin.org/2013/04/shooting-down-the-star-wars-myth/.

Polmar, Norman, and John D. Gresham. *Defcon-2: Standing on the Brink of Nuclear War during the Cuban Missile Crisis*. Hoboken, NJ: Wiley, 2006.

Reagan, Ronald. "Ronald Reagan's Announcement for Presidential Candidacy, 1979." Accessed January 5, 2025. https://www.reaganlibrary.gov/archives/speech/ronald-reagans-announcement-presidential-candidacy-1979.

Reagan, Ronald. "Reagan at 1980 Convention: Make America Great Again." Clip of Reagan convention speech, 1980. https://www.youtube.com/watch?v=FjkX_IBYQHw.

Reagan, Ronald. "Inaugural Address 1985." Ronald Reagan Presidential Library & Museum, January 21, 1985. https://www.reaganlibrary.gov/research/speeches/12185a.

Reagan, Ronald. "Ronald Reagan Second Inaugural Address." Bartleby, January 21, 1985b. https://www.bartleby.com/124/pres62.html.

Reagan, Ronald. "Star Wars Speech." Atomic Archive. Accessed 11-25-2024. http://www.atomicarchive.com/Docs/Missile/Starwars.shtml.

Bibliography

Reif, Kingston. "U.S. Nuclear Modernization Programs." Arms Control Association, August 2024. https://www.armscontrol.org/factsheets/USNuclearModernization.

Rhodes, Richard. *Arsenals of Folly: The Making of the Nuclear Arms Race.* New York: Alfred A. Knopf, 2007.

Scheer, Robert. "Former Defense Secretary Warns Civilization Is at Risk." Truthdig, September 1, 2017. https://www.truthdig.com/articles/former-defense-secretary-william-j-perry-on-the-nuclear-threat/.

Schurmann, Franz. *The Logic of World Power: An Inquiry into the Origins, Currents, and Contradictions of World Politics.* New York: Pantheon, 1974.

Selden, Mark. "A Forgotten Holocaust: U.S. Bombing Strategy, the Destruction of Japanese Cities, and the American Way of War from the Pacific War to Iraq." In *Bombing Civilians: A Twentieth-Century History,* edited by Yuki Tanaka and Marilyn B. Young, 77–96. New York: New Press, 2009.

Sherry, Michael S. *The Rise of American Air Power: The Creation of Armageddon.* New Haven, CT: Yale University Press, 1987.

Sherry, Michael S. *In the Shadow of War: The United States Since the 1930s.* New Haven, CT: Yale University Press, 1995.

Sherwin, Martin J. *A World Destroyed: Hiroshima and Its Legacies.* 3rd ed. Stanford, CA: Stanford University Press, 2003.

Smyth, Henry D. *Atomic Energy for Military Purposes.* Princeton, NJ: Princeton University, 1945.

Stimson, Henry Lewis. "The Decision to Use the Atomic Bomb." *Harper's Magazine,* February 1947. https://harpers.org/archive/1947/02/the-decision-to-use-the-atomic-bomb/.

Tanaka, Yuki. "British 'Humane Bombing' in Iraq During the Interwar Era." In *Bombing Civilians: A Twentieth-Century History*, edited by Yuki Tanaka and Marilyn B. Young, 8–29. New York: New Press, 2009.

Tanaka, Yuki, and Young Marilyn B., eds. *Bombing Civilians: A Twentieth-Century History*. New York: New Press, 2009.

Toland, John. *The Rising Sun: The Decline and Fall of the Japanese Empire, 1936, 1945*. Vol. 1. New York: Random House, 1970.

Trickey, Erick. "The Forgotten Story of the American Troops Who Got Caught Up in the Russian Civil War." *Smithsonian Magazine*, February 12, 2019. https://www.smithsonianmag.com/history/forgotten-doughboys-who-died-fighting-russian-civil-war-180971470/.

Truman, Harry. "Truman Statement on Hiroshima." Atomic Heritage Foundation, August 6, 1945. https://www.atomicheritage.org/key-documents/truman-statement-hiroshima.

Truman, Harry. "Harry S. Truman: 'The World Will Note That the First Atomic Bomb was Dropped on Hiroshima, a Military Base,' Radio Broadcast—1945." Speakola, August 9, 1945. https://speakola.com/political/harry-s-truman-radio-broadcast-1945.

Turse, Nick. "Empire of Bases." Voltaire Network, July 6, 2011. https://www.voltairenet.org/article170749.html.

U.S. Department of Energy. "Informing the Public." The Manhattan Project. Accessed January 5, 2025. https://www.osti.gov/opennet/manhattan-project-history/Events/1945-present/public_reaction.htm.

U.S. Department of Energy. "Average Annual Retail Fuel Price of Gasoline." Alternative Fuels Data Center. From Monthly Energy Review, June 2021. https://afdc.energy.gov/data/10641.

Bibliography

Vine, David, Deppen Patterson, and Leah Bolger. "Drawdown: Improving U.S. and Global Security Through Military Base Closures Abroad." Quincy Brief, no.16. Quincy Institute for Responsible Statecraft. September 2021. https://quincyinst.org/research/drawdown-improving-u-s-and-global-security-through-military-base-closures-abroad/#.

von Sponeck, Hans. "After the Journey—A UN Man's Open Letter to Tony Blair." New Statesman, September 23, 2010. https://www.gicj.org/about-us/executive-committee/positions-and-opinions-of-the-president/57-after-the-journey-un-mans-open-letter-to-tony-blair.

Weisman, Steven R. "Reagan Says Plan on Missile Defense Will Prevent War." *New York Times*, March 26, 1983. https://www.nytimes.com/1983/03/26/nyregion/reagan-says-plan-on-missile-defense-will-prevent-war.html.

Wellerstein, Alex. "The Demon Core and the Strange Death of Louis Slotin." *New Yorker*, May 21, 2016. https://www.newyorker.com/tech/annals-of-technology/demon-core-the-strange-death-of-louis-slotin.

Werrell, Kenneth P. *Death from the Heavens: A History of Strategic Bombing*. Annapolis, Maryland: Naval Institute Press, 2009.

Williams, Denton. "The Missouri Compromise." Truman Library Institute, August 1, 2024. https://www.trumanlibraryinstitute.org/the-missouri-compromise/.

Witner, Lawrence S. "The Nuclear Freeze and Its Impact." Arms Control Association. Accessed January 5, 2025. https://www.armscontrol.org/act/2010-12/nuclear-freeze-and-its-impact.

Wolfe, Alan. *The Rise and Fall of the 'Soviet Threat': Domestic Sources of the Cold War*. Washington DC: Institute for Policy Studies, 1979.

"The Yalta Declaration by the U.S.-U.K.-U.S.S.R. Yalta, Crimea, U.S.S.R. February 13, 1945. https://millercenter.org/the-presidency/presidential-speeches/february-11-1945-joint-statement-churchill-and-stalin-yalta.

Bibliography

See also "Communiqué Issued at the End of the Yalta Conference." https://history.state.gov/historicaldocuments/frus1945Berlinv02/d1417.

Yergin, Daniel. *Shattered Peace: The Origins of the Cold War.* New York: Penguin Books, 1990.

ENDNOTES

CHAPTER 1

1 Williams, "The Missouri Compromise."
2 Sherwin, *World Destroyed*, 146–150.
3 Sherwin, 146.
4 Alperovitz, *Atomic Diplomacy*, 181–182.
5 Alperovitz, 277.
6 "Yalta Declaration."
7 Alperovitz, *Atomic Diplomacy*, 62.
8 Alperovitz, 82.
9 Alperovitz, 62.
10 Sherwin, *World Destroyed*, 157–158.
11 Alperovitz, *The Decision to Use the Atomic Bomb*, 105.
12 Sherwin, 143.
13 Alperovitz, *Atomic Diplomacy*, 78.
14 Trickey, "Russian Civil War."
15 Alperovitz, *Atomic Diplomacy*, 81.
16 Alperovitz, 81.
17 Alperovitz, 88.
18 Messer, *End of an Alliance*, 13.
19 Messer, 68.
20 Alperovitz, *The Decision to Use the Atomic Bomb*, 207.
21 Alperovitz, 212–214.
22 Alperovitz, *Atomic Diplomacy*, 105.
23 Alperovitz, 106.
24 Alperovitz, 108.
25 Alperovitz, 5.
26 Alperovitz, 112.
27 Alperovitz, 120–126.
28 Alperovitz, 11–12.
29 Alperovitz, 38.

30   Alperovitz, 57.

31   Alperovitz, 246–247.

32   Alperovitz, 243.

33   Alperovitz, 491.

34   Alperovitz, *Atomic Diplomacy*, 199.

35   Alperovitz, *The Decision to Use the Atomic Bomb*, 383–389.

36   Alperovitz, 386.

37   Alperovitz, 387–389.

38   Messer, *End of an Alliance*, 114.

39   Alperovitz, *Atomic Diplomacy*, 230.

40   Alperovitz, *The Decision to Use the Atomic Bomb*, 382.

41   Alperovitz, 382.

42   Alperovitz, 242.

43   Alperovitz, 233.

44   Messer, "New Evidence on Truman's Decision," 21.

45   Messer, *End of an Alliance*, 105.

46   Messer, "New Evidence on Truman's Decision," 21.

47   Messer, *End of an Alliance*, 103.

48   Messer, "New Evidence on Truman's Decision," 20.

49   Alperovitz, *Atomic Diplomacy*, 158.

50   Hatano, "Atomic Bomb," 98.

51   Hatano.

52   Hatano.

53   Hasegawa, "Soviet Invasion," 121.

54   Hatano, "Atomic Bomb," 99.

55   Hatano.

56   Hatano, 100.

57   Hasegawa, "Soviet Invasion," 3.

58   Hatano, "Atomic Bomb," 100.

59   Hasegawa, "Soviet Invasion," 136.

60   Hatano, "Atomic Bomb," 101.

61   Hatano, 103.

62   Hatano, 104–106.

63   Frank, "Ketsu Gō," 90.

64   Frank, 90.

65   Hasegawa, "Soviet Invasion," 122.

66   Hasegawa, 119–120.

67   Hasegawa, 144.

68 Hatano, "Atomic Bomb," 111.

69 Hatano, 112.

70 Hatano.

71 Hasegawa, "Soviet Invasion," 143–144.

72 Alperovitz, *The Decision to Use the Atomic Bomb*, 59.

73 Alperovitz, 656

74 Office of the Historian, "Foreign Relations of the United States."

75 Bernstein, "Perils and Politics," 20–23.

76 Alperovitz, *Atomic Bomb*, 344–345.

77 Alperovitz, 355–356.

78 Alperovitz, 353.

79 Bernstein, "Atomic Bombings Reconsidered," 138.

80 Alperovitz, *The Decision to Use the Atomic Bomb*, 475.

81 Alperovitz, 277.

82 Sherwin, *World Destroyed*, 202.

83 Sherwin, 145.

84 Sherwin, 111.

85 Sherwin, 71.

86 Sherwin, 71–74.

87 Sherwin, 80.

88 Sherwin, 76.

89 Sherwin, 73.

90 Sherwin, 84.

91 Sherwin, 83.

92 Sherwin, 85–86.

93 Sherwin, 76.

94 Sherwin, 88–89.

95 Gaddis, *Cold War*, 24–25.

96 Sherwin, *World Destroyed*, 88.

97 Sherwin.

98 Sherwin, 89.

99 Gaddis, *Cold War*, 25–27.

100 Sherwin, *World Destroyed*, 114.

101 Alperovitz, *The Decision to Use the Atomic Bomb*, 524.

Chapter 2

1 Alperovitz, *The Decision to Use the Atomic Bomb*, 526.

2 Sherry, *Creation of Armageddon*, 312.

3 Alperovitz, *Atomic Diplomacy*, 17.
4 Werrell, *Death from the Heavens*, 131.
5 Werrell, 140.
6 Frank, *Downfall*, 53.
7 Werrell, *Death from the Heavens*, 141.
8 Frank, *Downfall*, 50–51.
9 Frank, 62.
10 Frank, 63.
11 Sherry, *Creation of Armageddon*, 58.
12 Sherry, 116.
13 Sherry.
14 Harvard Pusey Library, "Where Disaster Strikes."
15 Sherry, *Creation of Armageddon*, 8.
16 Sherry, 13.
17 Werrell, *Death from the Heavens*, 19.
18 Sherry, *Creation of Armageddon*, 15.
19 Sherry, 16.
20 Tanaka, "British 'Humane Bombing,'" 8–29.
21 Sherry, *Creation of Armageddon*, 24.
22 Sherry, 29.
23 Sherry, 74.
24 Sherry, *Creation of Armageddon*, 49–52; see also MacIsaac, *Strategic Bombing*, 4–10.
25 MacIsaac, *Strategic Bombing*, 12–13.
26 Sherry, *Creation of Armageddon*, 153.
27 Sherry, 154.
28 Sherry, 154.
29 Sherry, 262.
30 Werrell, *Death from the Heavens*, 114.
31 Werrell.
32 Sherry, *Creation of Armageddon*, 260.
33 Sherry, 261.

CHAPTER 3

1 Sherry, *Creation of Armageddon*, 274.
2 Sherry, 275.
3 Sherry.
4 Sherry, 276.

5   Frank, *Downfall*, 72–76.

6   Sherry, *Creation of Armageddon*, 310.

7   Sherry.

8   Selden, "Forgotten Holocaust," 86.

9   Sherry, *Creation of Armageddon*, 288.

10   Sherry, 289.

11   Sherry, 290.

12   Sherry, 312.

13   Alperovitz, *The Decision to Use the Atomic Bomb*, 164.

14   Truman, Radio Broadcast.

15   Alperovitz, *Atomic Bomb*, 427.

16   Frank, *Downfall*, 134.

17   Alperovitz, *Atomic Bomb*, 438.

18   Alperovitz, 439.

19   Alperovitz, 443.

20   Alperovitz, 444–445.

21   Alperovitz, 448–457.

22   Alperovitz.

23   Alperovitz, 466.

24   MacEachin, "Final Months."

25   MacEachin.

26   Hasegawa, "Soviet Factor," 202.

CHAPTER 4

1   Messer, *End of an Alliance*, 107.

2   Messer, 115.

3   Messer.

4   Messer, 128.

5   Messer, 129–130.

6   Messer, 130.

7   Messer.

8   Alperovitz, *Atomic Diplomacy*, 260.

9   Alperovitz, 261.

10   Alperovitz.

11   Alperovitz, 264.

12   Messer, *End of an Alliance*, 136.

13   Messer, 92.

14   Herken, *Winning Weapon*, 5.

15   Messer, *End of an Alliance*, 132–133.

16   Messer, 134.

17   Messer.

18   Messer, 135.

19   Messer, 140.

20   Messer, 150–154.

21   Herken, *Winning Weapon*, 74–82, 84–86.

22   Herken, 88.

CHAPTER 5

1   Herken, *Winning Weapon*, 36.

2   Herken.

3   Herken, 39.

4   Herken, 38.

5   Herken, 100.

6   Herken.

7   Herken, 101.

8   Herken, 101.

9   Herken, 102–103.

10   Herken, 84.

11   Holloway, *Stalin and the Bomb*, 111–112, 176–177.

12   Herken, *Winning Weapon*, 199–120.

13   Herken, 124.

14   Herken, 124–125.

15   Herken, 127.

16   Herken, 125.

17   Herken, 127.

18   Herken, 129.

19   Herken, 130.

20   Herken, 133–134.

21   Herken, 134, 147.

22   Herken, 134.

CHAPTER 6

1   Herken, *Winning Weapon*, 98.

2   Herken, 149.

3   Herken.

4   Herken.
5   Herken, 159.
6   Herken, 159–160.
7   Herken, 160–161.
8   Herken, 161–162.
9   Herken, 167.
10   Herken, 155–156, 164.
11   Herken, 170.
12   Herken, 172.
13   Herken, 181.
14   Herken, 182.
15   Herken, 185.
16   Herken, 191.
17   Herken.

CHAPTER 7

1   Herken, *Winning Weapon*, 197–198.
2   Herken, 271.
3   Herken.
4   Herken, 269.
5   Herken, 282.
6   Herken.
7   Herken, 293–294.
8   Herken, 294.
9   Herken, 294–295.
10   Herken, 295.

CHAPTER 8

1   Holloway, *Stalin and the Bomb*, 88–90.
2   Holloway, 90.
3   Holloway, 106.
4   Holloway, 115.
5   Holloway.
6   Holloway.
7   Holloway, 131.
8   Holloway, 132.
9   Holloway, 133.

10 Holloway, 134.
11 Holloway, 172.
12 Holloway, 184–185.
13 Holloway, 193.
14 Holloway, 221–222.
15 Holloway, 222.
16 Smyth, "Atomic Energy."
17 U.S. Department of Energy, "Informing the Public."
18 Holloway, *Stalin and the Bomb*, 173.
19 Holloway, 183–184, 187.
20 Holloway, 178–180.
21 Smyth, *Atomic Energy.*
22 Holloway, *Stalin and the Bomb*, 203.
23 Holloway, 209.
24 Holloway, 210–211.
25 Holloway, 211.

CHAPTER 9

1 Herken, *Winning Weapon*, 251.
2 Herken, 258.
3 Herken, 259–260.
4 Cray, *General of the Army*, 648.
5 Herken, *Winning Weapon*, 260.
6 Herken, 259.
7 Holloway, *Stalin and the Bomb*, 260.
8 Holloway, 259.
9 Holloway, 259–260.
10 Holloway, 260.
11 Holloway, 425, note 49.
12 Herken, 256.

CHAPTER 10

1 Ellsberg, *Doomsday Machine*, 26.
2 Ellsberg, 29.
3 Ellsberg, 30.
4 Ellsberg, 45.
5 Ellsberg, 67.

6 Ellsberg, 73.

7 Ellsberg, 75.

8 Ellsberg, 45–46.

9 Ellsberg, 49.

10 Ellsberg, 320.

11 Ellsberg, 48.

12 Ellsberg, 50.

13 Ellsberg, 49–52.

14 Ellsberg, 53–55.

15 Ellsberg, 55–56.

16 Ellsberg, 58–59.

17 Ellsberg, 59.

18 Ellsberg, 60–61.

19 Ellsberg, 62.

20 Ellsberg, 62–63.

21 Ellsberg, 63.

22 Ellsberg, 94.

23 Ellsberg, 96.

24 Ellsberg.

CHAPTER 11

1 Ellsberg, *Doomsday Machine*, 186.

2 Ellsberg, 188.

3 Polmar and Gresham, *Defcon-2*, 187.

4 Polmar and Gresham, 189, 191.

5 Polmar and Gresham, 190.

6 Ellsberg, *Doomsday Machine*, 199.

7 McNamara, "War and Peace."

8 McNamara, *Fog of War.*

9 Ellsberg, *Doomsday Machine*, 208.

10 Polmar and Gresham, *Defcon-2*, 150.

11 Polmar and Gresham, 190.

12 Blanton, "Annals of Blinksmanship."

13 Ellsberg, *Doomsday Machine*, 205.

14 Ellsberg, 205–206

15 Ellsberg, 206.

16 Ellsberg.

17 Ellsberg.

18 Perkovich, "Terrifying Lessons."
19 Perkovich.
20 Perkovich.
21 Burr and Blanton, "Submarines of October."
22 Orlov, "Recollections of Vadim Orlov."
23 Ellsberg, *Doomsday Machine*, 215–216.
24 Orlov, "Recollections of Vadim Orlov."
25 Ellsberg, *Doomsday Machine*, 216–217.
26 Ellsberg, 217.
27 Dobbs, *One Minute to Midnight*, 258–265, 263–265.
28 Dobbs, 271–272.
29 Ellsberg, *Doomsday Machine*, 218.
30 Ellsberg, 221–222.

CHAPTER 12

1   Rhodes, *Arsenals of Folly*, 167.
2   Jones, Blanton, and Harper, "Declassified and For Real."
3   Jones, "Cold War Part III."
4   Jones, Blanton, and Harper, "Declassified and For Real."
5   Jones, Blanton, and Harper.
6   Jones, "Cold War Part III."
7   Jones, Blanton, and Harper, "Declassified and For Real."
8   Jones, "Cold War Part II."
9   Jones, Blanton, and Harper. "Declassified and For Real."
10 Rhodes, *Arsenals of Folly*, 167.
11 Jones, Blanton, and Harper, "Declassified and For Real."
12 Jones, "Cold War Part II."

CHAPTER 13

1   FitzGerald, *Way Out There*, 198.
2   Reagan, "Star Wars Speech."
3   Reagan.
4   FitzGerald, *Way Out There*, 210.
5   FitzGerald, 211.
6   FitzGerald, 217.
7   FitzGerald, 216.
8   FitzGerald, 218.

9   FitzGerald, 219.

10   FitzGerald, 219–220.

11   FitzGerald, 218.

12   FitzGerald, 56.

13   FitzGerald, 56.

14   FitzGerald, 44–45, 47.

15   FitzGerald, 57.

16   FitzGerald, 20.

17   FitzGerald, 20–21.

18   FitzGerald, 21.

19   Weisman, "Reagan Says."

20   FitzGerald, *Way Out There*, 208.

21   FitzGerald, 209.

22   FitzGerald, 23.

23   FitzGerald, 121–122.

24   FitzGerald, 123.

25   FitzGerald, 126, 141–142.

26   FitzGerald, 234–235.

27   FitzGerald, 241.

28   Reagan, "Inaugural Address."

29   FitzGerald, *Way Out There*, 242.

30   FitzGerald, 242–243.

31   FitzGerald, 246.

32   FitzGerald, 246–247.

33   FitzGerald, 246.

34   FitzGerald.

35   FitzGerald, 248.

36   FitzGerald, 249–250.

37   FitzGerald, 248.

38   Herken, *Cardinal Choices*, 202, 210.

39   Podvig, "Star Wars Myth."

40   Nuclear Weapons Freeze Campaign, "Call to Halt."

41   FitzGerald, *Way Out There*, 180–182.

42   FitzGerald, 181.

43   Witner, "Nuclear Freeze."

44   Witner.

45   FitzGerald, *Way Out There*, 191.

46   Witner, "Nuclear Freeze."

47 FitzGerald, *Way Out There*, 261.
48 FitzGerald, 259.
49 FitzGerald, 254.
50 FitzGerald, 254, 252, 253.
51 FitzGerald, 252.
52 FitzGerald, 262.
53 FitzGerald, 263–264.
54 FitzGerald, 264.

CHAPTER 14

1 FitzGerald, *Way Out There*, 266–268.
2 FitzGerald, 256.
3 FitzGerald, 257.
4 FitzGerald, 257–258.
5 FitzGerald, 257.
6 Podvig, "Did Star Wars Help."
7 Podvig.
8 Podvig.
9 Podvig.
10 Podvig.
11 Podvig.
12 FitzGerald, 303.
13 FitzGerald, 311–312.
14 FitzGerald, 310.
15 Atomic Heritage Foundation, "Reagan and Gorbachev."
16 FitzGerald, *Way Out There*, 312–313.
17 FitzGerald, 313.
18 FitzGerald, 310.
19 FitzGerald, 323.
20 FitzGerald, 324–325.
21 FitzGerald, 177–178.
22 FitzGerald, 325–326.
23 FitzGerald, 326.
24 FitzGerald, 327.
25 FitzGerald.
26 Gorbachev, *Political Report*, 27.
27 FitzGerald, *Way Out There*, 328–329.
28 FitzGerald, 329.

29   FitzGerald, 330–332.

30   FitzGerald, 347.

31   FitzGerald, 349–350.

32   FitzGerald, 351–352.

33   FitzGerald, 353.

34   FitzGerald.

35   FitzGerald, 354.

36   FitzGerald.

37   FitzGerald, 333.

38   FitzGerald, 364.

39   FitzGerald.

40   FitzGerald, 364–365.

41   FitzGerald, 374.

42   FitzGerald.

43   FitzGerald, 374–375.

44   FitzGerald, 375–376.

45   FitzGerald, 375.

46   FitzGerald, 372.

47   FitzGerald, 377.

48   FitzGerald, 378.

49   FitzGerald, 389.

50   FitzGerald, 388–389.

51   FitzGerald, 404.

52   FitzGerald, 405.

53   FitzGerald, 405–406.

54   FitzGerald, 406.

55   FitzGerald, 407.

56   FitzGerald, 427–428.

57   FitzGerald, 430–431.

58   FitzGerald, 436.

59   FitzGerald.

60   FitzGerald, 438.

61   FitzGerald, 458.

62   FitzGerald, 457.

63   Podvig, "Star Wars Myth."

64   FitzGerald, *Way Out There*, 452.

CHAPTER 15

1 Albright, Interview by Matt Lauer
2 Chomsky, "Rollback - Part I."
3 Freedman, "After the Cold War."
4 Reagan, "Star Wars Speech."
5 Global Policy Forum, "Iraq Sanctions." See also Nagy, "Iraq Water Treatment Vulnerabilities."
6 Albright, "Punishing Saddam."
7 von Sponeck, "After the Journey."
8 Albright, Interview by Matt Lauer.
9 Bacevich, *New American Militarism*, 19.
10 "James Madison: Birthday Quotes."
11 Bacevich, *New American Militarism*, 16.

CHAPTER 16

1 Bacevich, *New American Militarism*, 154.
2 Bacevich, 155.
3 Bacevich, 155–156.
4 Bacevich, 156–157.
5 Bacevich, 161.
6 Bacevich, 162.
7 Bacevich, 164–165.
8 Bacevich, 166.
9 Bacevich, 168.
10 Friedman, "Manifesto."
11 Friedman.
12 Bacevich, *New American Militarism*, 179–182.
13 History Maps, 1973 Oil Crisis.
14 Bacevich, *New American Militarism*, 100–102.
15 Carter, "Crisis of Confidence."
16 Carter.
17 Reagan, "Ronald Reagan's Announcement."
18 Bacevich, *New American Militarism*, 180.
19 Bacevich, 180–181.
20 Carter, "State of the Union."
21 Brennan, "Efficacy and Ethics."
22 Calleo, *Follies of Power*, 77.

23   Becker and Shane, "Secret 'Kill List'"; see also Friedersdorf, "Obama Administration's Drone-Strike."

CHAPTER 17

1   National Priorities Project, "The Militarized Budget."
2   Sherwin, *World Destroyed*, 42.
3   Sherwin, 44.
4   Sherwin, 45.
5   Sherwin, 54.
6   Sherwin, 59–61.
7   Sherwin, 61–62.
8   Bush, *Science, the Endless Frontier.*
9   Bush, *Endless Horizons*, 88–89.
10   Bush, 98.
11   Dickson, *New Politics of Science*, 27, 119.
12   Dickson, 107.
13   Dickson, 109.
14   Dickson, 109–110.
15   Dickson, 113–114.
16   Dickson, 115.
17   Dickson, 102.
18   Rhodes, *Arsenals of Folly*, 140–141.
19   Rhodes, 142–143.
20   Rhodes, 141.
21   American Society of Civil Engineers, *Infrastructure Report Card.*

CHAPTER 18

1   Paltrow, "Special Report."
2   Paltrow.
3   Paltrow.
4   Scheer, "Civilization Is at Risk."
5   Paltrow, "Special Report."
6   Paltrow.
7   Kristensen et al, "Nuclear Force Modernization."
8   Kristensen et al.
9   Ellsberg, *Doomsday Machine*, 319–322.
10   Ellsberg, 320.

11   Ellsberg, 327.
12   Ellsberg, 321.
13   Ellsberg, 320.
14   Ellsberg, 311.
15   Ellsberg, 312.
16   Ellsberg, 322.
17   Kristensen et al, "Nuclear Force Modernization."
18   Mills, *Power Elite*, 184.
19   Cockburn, "Start a Nuclear War."
20   Cockburn.
21   Cockburn.
22   Cockburn.

Chapter 19

1   Dyson, *Disturbing the Universe*, 91.
2   Wellerstein, "Demon Core."
3   Davis, *Lawrence and Oppenheimer*, 250.
4   Davis, 129–130.
5   Davis, 131.
6   Davis, 132.
7   Davis, 234–235.
8   Sherry, *Shadow of War*, 223.
9   Mosher, "India and Pakistan."
10   Ellsberg, *The Doomsday Machine*, 129–135.
11   Ellsberg, 80–82; 114–118.
12   Ellsberg, 117.
13   Allison and Zelikow, *Essence of Decision*, 4.
14   Allison and Zelikow, 4–5.
15   Allison and Zelikow, 24.
16   Allison and Zelikow, 14.
17   Allison and Zelikow, 143.
18   Allison and Zelikow, 208–214.
19   Allison and Zelikow, 213–214.
20   Dower, *War without Mercy*, 137.
21   Dower, 137–138.
22   Quoted in Sherwin, *A World Destroyed*, 89.
23   Davis, *Lawrence and Oppenheimer*, 233.

.

INDEX

Index

Index

Index

and Conant, 28
meeting with Churchill, 28
Quebec agreement, 29
relationship with Stalin, 3
Saudi oil and, 162
U.S. as policeman of
the world, 184
Royall, Kenneth, 86
Russia
hypersonic cruise missiles, 181
New Strategic Arms Treaty, 174
threat of U.S. conventional
forces, 151–152
See also Soviet Union
Russo-Japanese War, 14, 49, 79

S

Saudi Arabia, 150, 161, 162
Savitsky, Valentin, 110
Schell, Jonathan, 128
Schelling, Thomas, 187
Schlesinger, James, 141
Sengier, Edgar, 60, 61, 69
Sherry, Michael, 37, 39, 40, 41
Sherwin, Martin J., viii, 4
Shigenori, Tōgō, 9, 17, 18, 19, 20, 21
Shultz, George, 132–134, 135–136,
137, 139–140, 142, 149
Slotin, Louis, 183, 194–195
Smyth, Henry DeWolf, 82
Smyth Report, 82–83
Soemu, Toyoda, 17, 19
Soviet Union
Anti-Ballistic Missile
(ABM) Treaty, 133
arms race, xi, 8, 27,
133–134, 139–140
atomic bomb project of, 77–85
atomic bomb test, 86
Balkan states and, 52–53
Berlin Blockade, 86–88, 176

breakup of, 148–150
Cheliabinsk, 81, 83–84
Cuban Missile Crisis,
101–113, 186–189, 192
entering war against Japan,
2, 9, 13, 16, 18, 21, 79
exclusion from Potsdam
Declaration, 28
ideological assault on science, 84
Manhattan Project
espionage, 63–65
NATO war simulation, 114–115
negotiations with China, 14
nomenklatura, 172
outsized defense budget, 170–171
perestroika, 148
Potsdam Declaration and, 13, 17
reclaiming Japanese
territory, 2, 14, 49, 79
Soviet submarines, 109–111
Sputnik, 169
Strategic Defense Initiative
and, 126, 134–135
troops on Iranian border, 177
uranium sources, 61–62, 77, 81
Western Europe invasion, 72–73
See also Gorbachev, Mikhail
Spaatz, General Carl, 25
Speakes, Larry, 140, 142
Sputnik, 169
Stalin, Joseph
Berlin Blockade, 87–88
distrust of Truman, 5
informed about the bomb, 11–12
reasons to distrust, 4
relationship with Roosevelt, 3
on scientific intelligentsia, 84, 85
Stalin and the Bomb
(Holloway), 77, 78–79
Star Wars Program. *See* Strategic
Defense Initiative (SDI)
Stettinius, Edward, 4, 7

.